alba house
DIVISION OF THE SOCIETY OF ST. PAUL
STATEN ISLAND, N.Y. 10314

THE LITERARY GENRE

Midrash

ADDISON G. WRIGHT, S.S.

Nihil Obstat:

Donald A. Panella, M.A., S.T.L., S.S.L.

Censor Deputatus

Imprimatur:

✝ Terence J. Cooke, D.D., V.G.

New York, N.Y. — March 30, 1967

Library of Congress Catalog Number: 67-24920

TO MY FATHER

Preface

"*H*e's one of those midrash people!" said an irate theologian in the days just before the Second Vatican Council. The man thus labeled was a Catholic writer on New Testament topics. One wonders what a Jewish listener might have made of the indictment, for such it was. He might suppose a preaching method, or a fund of stories and maxims, borrowed from the rabbis of the Middle Ages; that would be midrash, true enough. But what was meant was, that the writer in question was so benighted from the speaker's standpoint as to suppose that midrash, not unworthy of the Holy Spirit, was present to some degree in both the Old Testament and the New as well. The seemingly unforgivable presupposition lay in applying literary criticism to the New Testament books.

Happily, Father Wright has no need, in the pages that follow, to define or to defend "midrash people," whatever they might be. Even as he worked on the timely question that is his subject here, the Council was again making it explicit that for the progress of Biblical studies, "those who search out the intention of the sacred writers must, among other things, have regard for 'literary forms'" (*On Divine Revelation*, III, 12). Not long before, with the approval of Pope Paul VI, the Biblical Commission of the

Holy See had reiterated the charter for such studies within the Church provided by Pope Pius XII, and had applied it directly to the New Testament:

> The interpreter must be alert to the reminder given him by Pope Pius XII of happy memory when he charged him "to make judicious inquiry as to how far the form of expression or the type of literature adopted by the sacred writer may help towards the true and genuine interpretation, and to remain convinced that this part of his task cannot be neglected without great detriment to Catholic exegesis" (*Divino afflante*, EB 560).   In this reminder Pius XII of happy memory is laying down a general rule of hermeneutics, one by whose help the books both of the Old Testament and of the New are to be explained (*Instruction on the Historical Truth of the Gospels,* April 21, 1964, 1).

Where the resolute meeting of a challenge is present in the following pages is not in coping with the *malaise* of the occasional theologian, but in grappling with the subject itself.   Midrash is a technique of composition, and a form of literature, alien to our day.   It does not present, perhaps, the hazards to an appreciative understanding that are to be found in apocalyptic works, such as Daniel or the Apocalypse; but it has been far less studied, particularly in its relationship to the New Testament writings.   And if there are identifiable strands of midrashic text in the tapestry of the Word of God, it is important to know what they contribute to the overall design.

Father Wright is a skillful literary critic, meeting in this volume an immediate need of Biblical studies in our day.   Many who tell us there is midrash in the Bible would be hard put to it to tell us in what it consists, or what it shows us about the purposes and the message of its author; yet these are the essential questions, after all. Where in the Bible is midrash to be found? — the answers are nearly as varied as the individuals who venture an opinion. There is no agreement whether midrash, in the Bible, is a literary genre of its own, or merely an incidental technique of composition. If it is a technique, in what does the technique consist: is it just the reassembling of scattered Biblical phrases in a new context to lend traditional overtones to a quite new theme? Can the early chapters of St. Matthew and St. Luke be called midrash, and will this help to explain their message? Such questions are current; and those who have no context for them may easily greet them with something of the alarm of the pre-conciliar theologian. It is the framework for appreciating midrash in the Bible in due proportion to its ultimate significance for the abiding message of the total Word of God that is the unique contribution of this book.

Patrick W. Skehan
The Catholic University of America

ACKNOWLEDGMENTS

This study first appeared in article form in the *Catholic Biblical Quarterly* (vol. 28 [1966] 105-138; 417-457) and I acknowledge with thanks the permission of the editor to make it available (with minor improvements) to a wider audience in book form.

I would like to take this opportunity to express my deep gratitude to Patrick W. Skehan for his invaluable guidance and sustaining interest during the writing of this study and to Roland E. Murphy, O. Carm., for the many helpful suggestions which he offered. I have benefited from their assistance at every stage.

Thanks are also due to the following for permission to reproduce copyrighted material: Yale University Press for *The Midrash on Psalms* by W. Braude; Basil Blackwell for *The Essene Writings from Qumran* by A. Dupont-Sommer; E. J. Brill for *Scripture and Tradition in Judaism* by G. Vermes; Soncino Press for *Midrash Rabbah* edited by H. Freedman and M. Simon; Harcourt, Brace and World for *Theory of Literature* by R. Wellek and A. Warren; Harvard University Press for L. Finkelstein's translation of the Midrash of the Passover Haggadah in the *Harvard Theological Review* of 1938.

I am grateful also to Ruth Frank for translation of material from modern Hebrew and to the Reverend John E. Ridgell and the Reverend Mr. Richard T. Lawrence for assistance in proofreading. The kindness of librarians at the Library of Congress, the New York Public Library and at the libraries of The Catholic University of America, of Yale University, of the Johns Hopkins University and of the Pontifical Biblical Institute in Rome is deeply appreciated.

A. G. W.

St. Mary's Seminary
Baltimore
May 1967

Contents

ABBREVIATIONS

BA — Biblical Archaeologist
BeO — Bibbia e Oriente
Bib — Biblica
BJRylL — Bulletin of the John Rylands Library
BO — Bibliotheca Orientalis
CBQ — Catholic Biblical Quarterly
CCD — The Holy Bible, Confraternity of Christian Doctrine
      Version
CD — The Cairo Damascus Document
DJD — Discoveries in the Judaean Desert
EB — Enchiridion Biblicum
EstBib — Estudios Bíblicos
ETL — Ephemerides Theologicae Lovanienses
GA — Genesis Apocryphon
HarvTR — Harvard Theological Review
HibbJ — Hibbert Journal
HUCA — Hebrew Union College Annual
ICC — International Critical Commentary
IDB — Interpreter's Dictionary of the Bible
IEJ — Israel Exploration Journal
JA — Josephus' Jewish Antiquities
JBL — Journal of Biblical Literature
JJS — Journal of Jewish Studies
JQR — Jewish Quarterly Review
JSemS — Journal of Semitic Studies
Jub — The Book of Jubilees
LAB — Pseudo-Philo's Liber Antiquitatum Biblicarum
LTK — Lexikon für Theologie und Kirche
LXX — Septuagint

MGWJ — Monatschrift für Geschichte und Wissenschaft
    des Judentums
MS(S) — Manuscript(s)
MT — Masoretic text
NT — New Testament
NTS — New Testament Studies
OT — Old Testament
Q — Qumrân cave
QL — Qumrân Literature
1QH — The Qumrân Hymns of Thanksgiving
1QM — Qumrân War Scroll
1QS — Qumrân Manual of Discipline
4QF1 — A (so-called) florilegium, Qumrân Cave 4
4QpIs[c] — A pesher on Isaiah, Qumrân Cave 4
4QpNah — Pesher on Nahum, Qumrân Cave 4
4QS — A version of the Qumrân Manual of Discipline from
    Cave 4
11QPs[a] — A Psalm Scroll, Qumrân Cave 11
RB — Revue Biblique
RGG — Die Religion in Geschichte und Gegenwart
RSR — Recherches de Science Religieuse
RevQum — Revue de Qumrân
RevScPhTh — Revue des Sciences Philosophiques et Théo-
    logiques
TZ — Theologische Zeitschrift
VD — Verbum Domini
VDBS — Vigouroux, Dictionnaire de la Bible, Supplément
Vulg — Vulgate
VT — Vetus Testamentum
ZAW — Zeitschrift für die alttestamentliche Wissenschaft
ZNW — Zeitschrift für die neutestamentliche Wissenschaft
The names of the biblical books are abbreviated as in CCD.

Introduction

*O*ne of the prominent characteristics of biblical studies in this century has been the careful and explicit attention given to the classification of literary genres. Literature has been classified into genres for various purposes at least since Plato and such classification has become a standard technique for the study of literature in some schools of literary criticism [1] and has found its way into biblical criticism especially through the work of Gunkel and Lagrange. [2] For Catholic exegetes the search for literary forms began in an effort to extricate biblical inerrancy from various difficulties, but the contemporary interest in genres is motivated also by a realization that genre classification is

---

1. For a brief history of genre study see I. Ehrenpreis, *The "Types Approach" to Literature* (New York, 1945) 1-60. Lengthier treatments can be found in the standard histories of literary criticism such as René Wellek's recently completed *History of Modern Criticism* (4 vols.; New Haven, 1955-65).

2. See for example K. Grobel, "Form Criticism," *IDB;* J. Prado, "La controversia sobre los géneros literarios bíblicos desde fines del siglo pasado hasta nuestros días," *Los géneros literarios de la Sagrada Escritura* (Barcelona, 1957); J. Levie, *The Bible, Word of God in Words of Men,* tr. S. H. Treman (London, 1961), see index "Scripture, literary forms in."

an aid to understanding the individual author in relation both to his social context and to literary techniques which he has used, modified or opposed, and that no work of literature can be understood correctly unless it is put into its proper literary focus in this way. Encouraged by ecclesiastical documents [3] and stimulated by the increasing amount of literature from the ancient Near East available for comparative purposes, this trend in biblical criticism has resulted in many valuable studies of such genres as history, prophecy, apocalyptic, wisdom literature, gospel, etc.

Within the past fifteen years in Christian biblical circles there has been a growing interest in the literary genre midrash in both OT and NT studies and a large number of biblical passages have been assigned to that category. Also the discoveries at Qumrân have raised the question of midrash as a possible designation for the biblical commentaries found there. These recent discussions have by and large attempted in a commendable manner to dispel the lingering ideas of Wellhausen that midrash is a synonym for fable, and to focus attention on some of the primary characteristics of this genre.

Unfortunately, however, as the situation has developed, it has become more and more evident that there is little agreement among authors on what the genre midrash really is. In the discussions of the Qumrân literature (QL) there has been a tendency among some to use the word in a very limited sense, to use the word only of rabbinic commentaries, and to classify a work as midrash only if it

---

3. *Divino Afflante Spiritu* (*EB*[2] 558-60), the Letter to Cardinal Suhard (*EB*[2] 577-81), the instruction *On the Historical Truth of the Gospels* (April 21, 1964), and the constitution *De revelatione* of Vatican II (ch. 3).

exhibits specific literary structures and/or methods of exegesis of the rabbinic midrashim. [4]   In biblical studies on the other hand the term midrash has been used in a very extended sense.   Renée Bloch in the article "Midrash" in the *Dictionnaire de la Bible, Supplément,* has defined rabbinic midrash as a homiletic reflection or meditation on the Bible which seeks to reinterpret or actualize a given text of the past for present circumstances. [5]   Then in her discussion of the biblical material her definition becomes much broader, and she classifies each of the following as midrash: historical works which gloss Scripture for instruction and edification (the word *midrāš* in Chr); [6] a meditation on history, tending to give to this history a relevance for contemporary preoccupations (Chr); [7] a reuse of traditional sacred texts with a religious reflection on their content and on the past to which they witness, making them relevant for the contemporary situation (Ez 16); [8] anthological style or

---

4. E.g., W. H. Brownlee, "Biblical Interpretation among the Sectaries of the Dead Sea Scrolls," *BA* 14 (1951) 76; K. Stendahl, *The School of St. Matthew* (Uppsala, 1954) 184-85, 189-94; K. Elliger, *Studien zum Habakuk-Kommentar vom Toten Meer* (Tübingen, 1953) 163-64; L. H. Silberman, "Unriddling the Riddle," *RevQum* 3 (1961) 323-35.

5. R. Bloch, "Midrash," *VDBS* 5, 1265-66.   Even for rabbinic midrash Bloch gives two definitions, for in discussing the rabbinic use of the word midrash she also states: "le terme midrash désigne une exégèse qui, dépassant le simple sens littéral, essaie de pénétrer dans l'esprit de l'Écriture, de scruter le texte plus profondément et d'en tirer des interprétations qui ne sont pas toujours immédiatement obvies" (cols. 1264-65).

6. *Ibid.,* 1264.

7. *Ibid.,* 1271.

8. *Ibid.,* 1272; cf. also R. Bloch, "Ézéchiel XVI: exemple parfait du procédé midrashique dans la Bible," *Cahiers Sioniens* 9 (1955) 193-223.

composition, "which is a reflection or meditation on prior texts that develops, enriches and transposes the earlier message" (Sir, Wis, Prv, 1QH, Lk 1-2, etc.); [9] constant reference to the biblical data, dramatization and reinterpretation of the events and aspirations of the age (Ct); [10] the use of scriptural texts for the purpose of edification in the light of contemporary needs (Sir 44, 1-50, 24); [11] a work which alludes to earlier history and suppresses, embellishes and rearranges the traditional accounts and imposes a new meaning on them (Wis 10-19); [12] a work with scriptural reminiscences which proceeds entirely from a meditation on Scripture (Sir 24); [13] a development on OT texts (Mt 1-2). [14] Mlle. Bloch also distinguishes between "*midrash* properly speaking" which begins with the Targum of Jerusalem and "*midrashic genre* as such" which is already present in the biblical literature, [15] but the terms are not explained nor is her use of them consistent. [16]

A number of exegetes have taken up one or another of the definitions of Mlle. Bloch and have enlarged upon her brief observations in the *Dictionnaire,* and many other writers have independently proposed examples of OT and

---

9. Bloch, *VDBS* 5, 1270-71, 1273, 1279.

10. *Ibid.,* 1273.

11. *Ibid.,* 1274.

12. *Ibid.*

13. *Ibid.,* 1273.

14. *Ibid.,* 1279; although in "Quelques aspects de la figure de Moïse dans la tradition rabbinique," *Cahiers Sioniens* 8 (1954) 283, she prefers to draw no conclusion on the literary form of Mt 1-2.

15. Renée Bloch, "Note méthodologique pour l'étude de la littérature rabbinique," *RSR* 43 (1955) 212.

16. For example she calls the Canticle "un pur midrash" (*VDBS* 5, 1273), Sir 44, 1-50, 24 "un midrash aggadique" (*ibid.,* 1274), etc.

NT midrash based on similar, and equally divergent, conceptions (midrash is the glossing of Sacred Scripture, the meditation on previous Scripture in the light of new events, the interpretation of events or themes or persons in the light of previous Scripture, the presentation of data in OT terms, embellished history, didactic fiction). [17] Even the sources underlying the Gospels and the Gospels themselves have been viewed as Christian midrashim (works made up of a series of OT texts each followed by its Christian explication), [18] and the redaction of OT texts has been suggested as the earliest example of midrash. [19] The result is that the word midrash at present is an equivocal term and is being used to describe a mass of disparate material. Indeed, if some of the definitions are correct, large amounts, if not the whole of the Bible, would have to be called midrash. Hence, the word as used currently in biblical studies

---

17. Anything like a complete listing would be impossible but typical and influential examples would be R. Laurentin, *Structure et théologie de Luc I-II* (Paris, 1957) 93-119; M. Bourke, "The Literary Genus of Matthew 1-2," *CBQ* 22 (1960) 160-75; P. Ellis, *The Men and the Message of the Old Testament* (Collegeville, 1963) 448-63, 515-29, 533-34; A. Robert et A. Feuillet, *Introduction à la Bible* (2 vols.; Tournai, 1957-59) see index, "midrash"; G. Auzou, *The Formation of the Bible*, tr. J. Thornton (St. Louis, 1963) 200, 207, 237-39, 244; A. Robert and A. Tricot, *Guide to the Bible*, tr. E. Arbez and M. R. P. McGuire, I (2d ed.; Tournai, 1960) 505-509; J. McKenzie, *Dictionary of the Bible* (Milwaukee, 1965) 574-76.

18. J. W. Doeve, "Le rôle de la tradition orale dans la composition des évangiles synoptiques," *La Formation des évangiles*, éds. J. Cambier et L. Cerfaux (Bruges, 1957) 70-84.

19. R. H. Pfeiffer, *Introduction to the Old Testament* (2d ed.; London, 1952) 309, 361, 368-73; G. Vermes, *Scripture and Tradition in Judaism* (Leiden, 1961) 127-77; Bloch, *VDBS* 5, 1273, 1275; S. Sandmel, "The Haggada Within Scripture," *JBL* 80 (1961) 105-122.

is approaching the point where it is no longer really meaningful and where some of the material designated as midrash
resembles the later rabbinic midrash only in a very super-
ficial way.   And surprisingly very few voices have been
raised in protest. [20]

The reasons for this confusion seem to be twofold.   First,
in the studies of rabbinic midrash written before Bloch's
article there had been no real attempt carefully to define
midrash as a literary form.   Studies of the rabbinic midrashim and other rabbinic literature were primarily interested
in the content, methods of exegesis and the dating of the
rabbinic materials. [21]   Definitions of midrash were offered
but they were largely non-technical and failed to sift primary
characteristics from secondary features—nor was there an

20. J. Coppens, "L'Évangile lucanien de l'enfance," *ETL* 33
(1957) 733; C. Spicq, "Nouvelles réflexions sur la théologie biblique,"
RevScPhTh 42 (1958) 218, n. 34; E. Galbiati, "Esegesi degli Evangeli
festivi. L'Adorazione dei Magi (Matt 2, 1-12)," *BeO* 4 (1962) 26.

21. E.g., L. Zunz, *Die gottesdienstlichen Vorträge der Juden*
(Frankfurt, 1832; 2d ed., 1892); A. Geiger, *Urschrift und Über-
setzungen der Bibel in ihrer Abhängigkeit von der innern Entwicklung
des Judenthums* (Breslau, 1857); H. L. Strack, *Einleitung in Talmud
und Midrasch* (5 editions 1887-1920; an English translation which
really is a sixth edition was published in 1931 [Philadelphia: Jewish
Publication Society] and reprinted in 1959 [New York: Meridian
Books]); W. Bacher, *Die exegetische Terminologie der jüdischen
Traditionsliteratur* (2 vols.; Leipzig, 1899-1905); *id., Die Agada der
Tannaiten* (2 vols.; Strassburg, 1884-90); *id., Die Agada der baby-
lonischen Amoräer* (Strassburg, 1878); *id., Die Agada der palä-
stinensischen Amoräer* (3 vols.; Strassburg, 1892-99); L. Ginzberg,
Legends of the Jews (7 vols.; Philadelphia, 1909-38); G. F. Moore,
Judaism in the First Centuries of the Christian Era (3 vols.; Cam-
bridge, 1927-30); J. Bonsirven, *Le Judaïsme palestinien au temps de
Jésus Christ* (2 vols.; Paris, 1935).   Also the pertinent articles in
The Jewish Encyclopedia, Encyclopaedia Judaica, and the introductions in the various editions of the midrashim.

imperative need to, since the studies were concerned not with midrash as a literary genre (i.e., with finding other material similar to the rabbinic and building up a classification), but with analyzing a given body of literature. Secondly, the real contribution of Mlle. Bloch to midrashic studies lay not in her delineation of the classification and definition of the genre but in her effort to point out the history of the genre, i.e., its biblical origins and its development through the biblical and post-biblical literature—something casually mentioned in the earlier works but never energetically pursued. [22]   The assumption underlying the earlier works had been that the period of great haggadic creativity had been between 100-500 A.D.   Between 1930-50, however, it became clear that the Palestinian Targum, including its midrashic elements, is older than the Targum Onkelos and is pre-Christian in date, [23] that a great number of haggadic interpretations figure in works such as the QL, Pseudo-Philo and Josephus and are therefore of pre-tannaitic origin, and it was suggested by A. Robert that the postexilic biblical phenomenon which he called *style anthologique* was the earliest form of the midrashic genre. [24]

---

22. Save to some extent in the remarkable pioneer works of Geiger and Zunz, *cit. sup.* n. 21.

23. P. Kahle, *Masoreten des Westens*, vol. 2 (Stuttgart, 1930) 9-13; *id., The Cairo Geniza* (London, 1947) 122-23; 2d ed. (Oxford, 1959) 191-208.—See M. McNamara, "Targumic Studies," *CBQ* 28 (1966) 1-19.

24. E.g., A. Robert "Les attaches littéraires bibliques de Prov. i-ix," *RB* 43 (1934) 42-68, 172-204, 374-84; 44 (1935), 344-65, 502-25; *id.*, "Le genre littéraire du Cantique des cantiques," *Vivre et Penser*, 3d series (1943-44) 192-213; *id.*, "Littéraires (genres)," *VDBS* 5, 411-17; *id.*, "Les genres littéraires," *Initiation Biblique*, éds. A. Robert et A. Tricot (3d éd. rev.; Paris, 1954) 305-309 (= *Guide to the Bible*, 2d ed., *cit. sup.*).

In other words, both the nature and the antiquity of haggadic midrash came to be seen in an entirely different perspective. There was the feeling that the moment was ripe for the elaboration of a new synthesis and Bloch attempted such an undertaking, although her tragic death in 1955 prevented her from doing much more than grapple with the preliminaries. [25] She of course realized that the formulation of this synthesis required a precise definition of midrash and she did isolate admirably some of the primary characteristics of the genre at the beginning of her article in the *Dictionnaire*. [26] But as we have seen, before her study comes to a close her definition becomes very broad indeed, and this undoubtedly out of a laudable desire to show the organic bond between the Bible and the later rabbinic literature.

It is not surprising, then, that we find a variety of definitions of midrash in current biblical and intertestamental studies, since the biblical or intertestamental scholar, increasingly desirous of accurately classifying his literature according to literary genres, and alerted to the possibility of midrash in his material by the work of Bloch or by

---

25. Cf. "Écriture et tradition dans le judaïsme, aperçus sur l'origine du midrash," *Cahiers Sioniens* 8 (1954) 9-34; "Note méthodologique pour l'étude de la littérature rabbinique," *RSR* 43 (1955) 194-227; "Note sur l'utilisation des fragments de la Geniza du Caire pour l'étude du Targum palestinien," *Revue des Études Juives*, N.S. 14 (1955) 5-35; "Midrash," *VDBS* 5, 1263-1281; "Ézéchiel XVI: exemple parfait du procédé midrashique dans la Bible," *Cahiers Sioniens* 9 (1955) 193-223; "Quelques aspects de la figure de Moïse dans la tradition rabbinique," *Cahiers Sioniens* 8 (1954) 211-85; "Juda engendra Pharès et Zarah de Thamar (Mt 1, 3)," *Mélanges bibliques rédigés en l'honneur de André Robert* (Paris, 1956) 381-89.

26. Cols. 1265-66.

the same new theories and data that occasioned the work of Bloch, is left to draw upon a wide variety of definitions from midrashic studies in which definitions either are not the main point of interest or are not the strongest feature. There is a real need, then, for an investigation into midrash as a literary form for the purpose of delineating its primary characteristics, constructing a definition in terms of them, and finding genuine pre-rabbinic examples. It is to this task that we have addressed ourselves in the following pages in the hope that we might offer some contribution to that area of midrashic studies which is of prime importance to the biblical scholar and which has been so long neglected.

Chapter 1
A Theory of Genre

S cholars are fairly well agreed today that there is no
one definition of "literary genre." Any shared characteristics are sufficient basis for putting two or more
works together, provided that these works are considered
as belonging together only in respect of these characteristics.
The classifier must, however, steadfastly keep in mind the
basis for his system, or he is likely to confuse more than he
clarifies.

Tradition is generally the basis for grouping literary
works. [1] As Bruce Vawter remarks in his study of apocalyptic:

However necessary, not to say indispensable, is our
determination of literary forms and interpretation ac-

---

1. On genre theory see Ehrenpreis, *op. cit.* (see Introduction, n.
1), 1-60; R. Wellek and A. Warren, *Theory of Literature* (3rd ed.;
New York, 1962) 226-37; L. Alonso-Schökel, "Genera litteraria," VD
38 (1960) 3-15; and the bibliography given in each.—Today the novel,
the short story, the play, the lyric poem, etc., are called *types*. Early
English critics called them *kinds*. In an effort to be precise and
to avoid confusion of terms, many scholars have adopted the French
term, *genre*, and scholarship in genres is sometimes known as
genology. The word *form* is also employed, especially in biblical
studies because of the influence of the terms *Formgeschichte* and
Form Criticism.

cording to their canons, we have to recognize that the determination and specification are really ours rather than the ancient writers'. The ancient writer was not precisely conscious of writing in a "literary form," aside, of course, from such obvious genres as prose or poetry, part of the mechanics common to all literatures. His lack of conscious advertence makes the literary forms no less definable and applicable, but it should also remind us that his own appreciation of his work ought to be consulted in forming the definition. What the writer was aware of was that he wrote within a particular tradition: it is this that largely decided the literary form to which we have given a name. He was a Deuteronomist, a priestly writer, a follower of the sages, an anthologist of the prophets, or the like. [2]

To the degree, then, that the precise traditions followed by a work can be ascertained, its classification is sure.

Traditions may be characterized by many different elements: plot, subject matter, versification, author's attitude, or any combination of these and other characteristics. Wellek and Warren write:

> Genre should be conceived, we think, as a grouping of literary works based, theoretically, upon both outer form (specific meter or structure) and also upon inner form (attitude, tone, purpose—more crudely, subject and audience). The ostensible basis may be one or the other (e.g., "pastoral" and "satire" for the inner form; dipodic verse and Pindaric ode for outer); but

---

2. B. Vawter, C.M., "Apocalyptic: Its Relation to Prophecy," *CBQ* 22 (1960) 33.

the critical problem will then be to find the *other* dimension, to complete the diagram .... In general, our conception of genre should lean to the formalistic side, that is, incline to generize Hudibrastic octosyllabics or the sonnet rather than the political novel or the novel about factory workers: we are thinking of "literary" kinds, not the subject-matter classifications as might equally be made for non-fiction. [3]

A single work rarely embodies all the conventions which, through the centuries, have characterized one or another of the many examples of a genre. In fact, the complex of conventions of which a genre consists is not at all stable. From time to time some elements may be changed, dropped, or added as individual writers express themselves within a tradition under the influence of various other traditions. One of the least constant ingredients is the name of the genre, as the terms *elegy* and *movies* suggest. On the one hand, a genre may have had as many different names (signifying variously the form, the medium, and the place of performance) as the movies, photoplay, screenplay, cinema, motion picture, or nickelodeon. On the other hand, a single name, the elegy, may have been attached to such different genres as all poems in the elegiac meter, reflective poems in a serious mood regardless of meter, poems on death, or musical compositions of pensive or mournful mood. Irene Behrens has shown that while epic, drama, and lyric may have existed from antiquity, none of them has retained the same name for the same genre. [4]   It is also possible for

3. Wellek and Warren, *op. cit.*, 231-33.
4. I. Behrens, *Die Lehre von der Einteilung der Dichtkunst* (Halle, 1940) 221 and *passim*.

a word to have had a non-technical usage before becoming the name of a genre. As Vawter observes in the same article on apocalyptic:

> In 1, 1 the author of Ap applies the term *apokalypsis* to his work. It is apparent that the term is used by him in no technical way, but not only have we made it the title of his book, we have extended it to a broad body of mainly Jewish literature with which his book shares some striking characteristics .... [5]

Genres, then, are literary traditions or institutions within which authors shape their materials, but these traditions, being complex, interwoven and developing, require on our part a precise and scientific description and delineation if our classification of the works in those traditions is to be of intelligible value. And the categories that we form as we look back over the history of a genre from our present vantage point may well be different from those of earlier times.

> Do genres remain fixed? Presumably not. With the addition of new works, our categories shift. Study the effect on theory of the novel of *Tristram Shandy* or *Ulysses.* When Milton wrote *Paradise Lost,* he thought of it as one with the *Iliad* as well as the *Aeneid;* we would doubtless sharply distinguish oral epic from literary epic, whether or not we think of the *Iliad* as the former. Milton probably would not have granted that the *Faerie Queene* was an epic, though written in a time when epic and romance were still unseparate and when the allegorical character of epic was held dominant; yet

---

5. *Art. cit.*, 33.

Spenser certainly thought of himself as writing the kind of poem Homer wrote. [6]

The strictness of our classifications will vary with the criteria which the classifier assigns to each genre. The realm of the sonnet, for example, is restricted or expanded as one does or does not require a special relationship between the octave and the sestet, or between the three quatrains and the couplet. Whether the limits of a genre are to be severe or flexible depends on the general reason for using the arrangement. If a biographer is considering the effect of the epic tradition upon Milton, he will probably adopt Milton's own interpretation of that tradition. If an historian of the drama finds that the classical drama of France followed a set of very precise rules, he will modify his own terms in dealing with French plays and not assume Greek or Roman standards. And if an historian of midrash wishes to demonstrate the continuity of rabbinic midrash with the Bible he will perhaps define the genre in terms of the whole tradition back to the first implicit citation of Scripture by a writer, but the literary critic may adopt a more limited definition so as to delineate really similar groups of literature.

Each genre presents its own unique problems of research for the critic due to the way it has developed historically and due to the critical work that has preceded and contributed to the modern concept of the genre. In the case of midrash it seems best to start with a history of the name of the genre in its technical and non-technical usages.

---

6. Wellek and Warren, *op. cit.*, 227.

Chapter 2
The Name Midrash

*7*he English word midrash is a transliteration of the Hebrew noun *midrāš* whose first extant occurrences are in 2 Chr where it appears twice as the title of a literary work: [1] "The rest of the acts of Abijah, his ways and his sayings, are written in the Midrash of the prophet Iddo" (2 Chr 13, 22); "As for his [Joash'] sons, the many oracles against him, and the rebuilding of the Temple, these are written in the Midrash of the Book of the Kings" (2 Chr 24, 27). What the Chronicler meant by the term *midrāš* has remained a matter of dispute to this day. From the way the works are cited they evidently contained some historical material, but how it was presented and its relation to the material in Sm-Kgs cannot be ascertained. The books of Chronicles themselves would be our only source of information and it is in no way clear to what extent the Chronicler excerpted from these works or to what extent he may have modified that material. It is certainly gratuitous to say that the Chronicler acquired his method of historio-

---

1. Noth, Galling, Torrey, Pfeiffer and others deny the existence of these works cited by the Chronicler and see them as a parading of authorities, but the majority of commentators accepts them as real works and ones that the Chronicler utilized.

graphy from the Midrash, as Driver suggests. [2] Furthermore, we cannot even be sure if the Midrash of the Book
of the Kings is the only title the book had, or if the Midrash
of the Prophet Iddo is a separate work or only a section of
the Midrash of the Book of the Kings. [3]

Many have tried to work back to the meaning of *midrāš*
through the word itself. Some have assumed that the word
in Chr has the later technical, rabbinic acceptation and that
it designates an imaginative development of a Scriptural text
(Kgs) along didactic, homiletic and edifying lines. [4] This
of course is precisely the thing to be proven and is now
rendered most unlikely by the varied and non-technical
usage of *midrāš* in the QL (see below). Others, arguing
from the meaning of the stem, propose that *midrāš* means
"meditation" on Kgs, [5] or "explanation, commentary" on
Kgs, [6] but there is no evidence that the stem bears the latter

---

2. S. R. Driver, *An Introduction to the Literature of the Old
Testament* (10th ed.; New York, 1903) 534-35.

3. Most commentators are of the opinion that "The Midrash of
the Book of the Kings" is identical with "The Book of the Kings of
Israel" cited in 2 Chr 20, 34, "The Acts of the Kings of Israel
and Judah" (2 Chr 33, 18), "The Book of the Kings of Israel
and Judah" (1 Chr 9, 1; 2 Chr 27, 7; 35, 27; 36, 8), and "The Book
of the Kings of Judah and Israel" (2 Chr 16, 11; 25, 26; 28, 26;
32, 32). The Chronicler cites sixteen other works, including "The
Midrash of the prophet Iddo," and some would see many of these
as sections of "The Book (Midrash of the Book/Acts) of the Kings"
(Curtis-Madsen, Rudolph, Goettsberger, Eissfeldt, Bentzen).

4. Driver, *op. cit.*, 529, and the many who follow him; E. Pode-
chard, "Les références du Chroniqueur," *RB* 12 (1915) 239-41;
Zunz, *op. cit.*, 38; R. Bloch, *VDBS* 5, 1264 (the probability).

5. A. M. Brunet, "Paralipomènes," *VDBS* 6, 1236-37.

6. R. North, *Israel's Chronicle* (1st prelim. ed. mimeogr.; St.
Mary's, Kansas, 1963) 345-55: a collection of explanations or facts
gradually found needful or interesting at the side of the Kgs narrative.

meaning at this time [7] and the relationship to Kgs is certainly not reflected in the other titles the book seems to have. [8]   Others, following LXX,[9] suggest the word means

---

7. In the OT the verb *dāraš* means basically "to seek" and from this other shades of meaning have developed: "inquire, investigate, beseech, demand, require, avenge, pursue, promote, take care of, search, seek out, examine and study." The verb occurs in the sense of "study" in Ps 111, 2; Eccl 1, 13, and is applied in this sense to the study of a text in Ezr 7, 10 and Sir 32, 15 ("study of the Law"). A case could be made for the argument that *dāraš* in Ezr already means "interpret" (as it clearly does at Qumrân) for biblical interpretation was certainly being practiced then. But it seems safer to assign the meaning "study" and to assume that the semantic change in the term's meaning ("study" to "interpret") was the outcome of such practice and not its forerunner.—For a study of the words *dāraš* and *midrāš* see M. Gertner, "Terms of Scriptural Interpretation: A Study in Hebrew Semantics," *Bulletin of the School of Oriental and African Studies, University of London* 25 (1962) 1-27.

8. See n. 3 above.

9. 2 Chr 13, 22:

> MT: *ketûbîm bemidraš hannābî' 'iddô*
> LXX: *gegrammenoi epi bibliō tou prophētou Adō*
> be[2]: *gegrammenoi epi bibliou en tē ekzētēsei Addōk tou prophētou*
> Vulg: *scripta sunt diligentissime in libro Addo prophetae*

2 Chr 24, 27:

> MT: *ketûbîm 'al-midraš sēper hammelākîm*
> LXX: *gegrammena epi tēn graphēn tōn basileōn*
> be[2]: *gegrammena (-oi e[2]) epi tēn graphēn bibliou tōn basileōn*
> Vulg: *scripta sunt diligentius in libro regum*

Minuscules be[2] for 2 Chr represent a proto-Lucianic stage of Greek OT revision, probably toward the end of the 1st cent. B.C. (cf. D. Barthélemy, *Les dévanciers d'Aquila* [VTSuppl 10; Leiden, 1963] 41-42, 47, 51, 62, 67 for 2 Chr; and the remarks of F. M. Cross, "The History of the Biblical Text in the Light of Discoveries in the

"book, essay, study," [10] but this fits poorly in 24, 27 where "book" is already in the Hebrew text. [11] Zeitlin points out the frequent use of *drš* in the OT in the meaning of "inquire (of a prophet)" and concludes that a *midrāš* was a book in which were recorded the inquiries of the kings and the answers and explanations of the seers and prophets. [12] However, according to 2 Chr "The Midrash of the Prophet Iddo" is made up at least partly of "the rest of the acts of Abijah, and his ways and his sayings" (13, 22) and "The Midrash of the Book of the Kings" contains not only the oracles against Joash but also information on his sons and on the rebuilding of the temple (24, 27). This does not exclude Zeitlin's concept of the work, but it indicates that the Midrash was not simply a book of questions and answers, nor valued primarily as such. Fol-

---

Judaean Desert," *HarvTR* 57 [1964] 295). *Ekzētēsei* in be[2] is used as a mechanical equivalent of *midrāš* and perhaps was an equivalent in common usage (cf. 1 Tim 1, 4; Gertner, *art. cit.*, 13). The fact that it is used only in 13, 22 in connection with the prophet and not in 24, 27 suggests that the revisers may have understood *midrāš* in 13, 22 as a book of prophetic responses or biblical interpretations. Jerome apparently understood *midrāš* as a process in both occurrences.

10. Goettsberger; Galling; Rudolph; Bacher, *Terminologie,* I, 104; O. Eissfeldt, *The Old Testament, An Introduction,* tr. P. Ackroyd (Oxford, 1965) 534.

11. Eissfeldt suggests that *sēper* in 24, 27 is a gloss for clarification for it is not represented in LXX. Bacher admits this as a possibility while also suggesting that *midrāš sēper* is a pleonasm (cf. *mᵉgillat sēper*: Jer 36, 2; Ez 2, 9; Ps 40, 8) rendered with one word by LXX and thus the change from *biblion* (13, 22) to *graphē* in 24, 27. From LXX one might wonder if *midrāš* is not the later gloss except for the fact that *graphē* is never used to render *sēper* in LXX.

12. S. Zeitlin, "Midrash: A Historical Study," *JQR* NS 44 (1953) 24-25.

lowing Zeitlin's lead, Gertner has proposed that *midrāš* in Chr means "narrative" or "account," concepts for which there were no adequate terms in biblical Hebrew. The noun *mispār* on one occasion means "narrative" (Jgs 7, 15) but would not do for the work in Chr which was, according to Gertner, an account of prophecies as well as of historical events, and consequently *midrāš* was used to cover both elements. The root *drš* therefore would already have assumed the connotation of "conveyance" before it came to mean "interpretation," and Gertner points out that this combination of "interpretation" and "narrative" in a single word is paralleled in the corresponding Greek and Latin terms *'ermēneia, exēgēsis, expositio* and *interpretatio.* [13]   This would be an attractive theory, if it were not for the facts that it is only later in the rabbinic period that we have evidence for *drš* with any note of conveyance (*drš* meaning "to preach," "to recite a midrash") and that, in view of the basic meaning of the stem ("to seek"), it is hard to imagine *drš* developing that meaning before it meant "interpret." In fine, none of the theories on the meaning of *midrāš* in Chr is without at least apparent difficulties and there is no real basis available yet for deciding between them.

The only other occurrence of *midrāš* in the OT is in the alphabetic canticle which ends the work of Ben Sira:

> Turn to me, you who need instruction
> And lodge in my house of midrash (school).
>
> *p^enú 'ēlay s^ekālîm*
> *w^elînû b^ebêt midrāšî* (Sir 51, 23).

This is the first occurrence of the technical term *bêt-ham-*

---

13. Gertner, *art. cit.*, 10-11; also G. Rinaldi, "Alcuni termini ebraici relativi alla letteratura," *Bib* 40 (1959) 277.

midrāš, common in later Hebrew as a designation of a rabbinical school for the study of the Scriptures, and because of its early appearance here, Israel Lévi suggests that it is a later interpolation and that the original probably read *bêt mûsār*. [14]   The mere fact that this would be the earliest occurrence of the expression does not make its appearance here intrinsically impossible, but there is much to be said in favor of Lévi's suggestion on other grounds. [15]   However, even if the reading is original, the occurrence is of little importance here since the word *midrāš* is not being used as a literary term, [16] nor does it necessarily indicate that the word at this time connotes the activity of biblical interpretation; the noun could merely mean "study."

THE WORD *Midrāš* IN THE QUMRAN LITERATURE

The word *midrāš* has occurred five times to date in the published QL and four additional occurrences are reported

---

14. Israel Lévi, *L'Ecclésiastique ou la sagesse de Jésus, fils de Sira*, II (Paris, 1901) 229.   Others accept it as original.

15. First of all the suffix (*midrāšî*) is not reflected in the Greek (*en oikō paideias*) or in the Syriac (*bêt yulpânâ'*)—a minor point but one providing a slight cause for doubt.   Secondly, the Greek *paideia* is almost a strict equivalent of *mûsār* not only in meaning but also in LXX usage.   Moreover, the fact that our Hebrew text of this canticle is a medieval reworking is now clear from 11Q Psᵃ; cf. J. A. Sanders, *The Psalms Scroll of Qumrân Cave 11* (*DJD* 4; Oxford, 1965) 79-85.

16. The appearance of this canticle in 11Q Psᵃ as a psalm of David seems to indicate that it is a work independent of Sir (cf. Sanders, *op. cit.*, 83).   However, it is still possible, as some have suggested, that the phrase *bêt-midrāšî* in its context in Sir is intended to refer to Ben Sira's book and not to a school, but the use would be figurative.

in unpublished material from Cave 4. The noun means "juridical investigation" (1QS 6, 24, and probably in 1QS 8, 26), "study" (of the law: 1QS 8, 15), and "interpretation" (of the law: CD 20, 6, and in two unpublished MSS of CD from Cave 4 [17]). It is also used as the title of a *pēšer* on the first lines of Pss 1 and 2 (4QF1 1, 14) where it seems to have the generic meaning of "interpretation, exposition." [18] It occurs again as a title in fragments of two MSS of the Manual of Discipline from 4Q which reveal a text differing little from 1QS except for col. 5. In this column the two MSS present a form that is shorter and more primitive than the one we already possessed and they furnish this reading for the first line of the column: *mdrš lmśkyl 'l 'nšy htwrh hmtndbym* [19] ("A midrash for [of ?] [20] the instructor concerning the men of the law who dedicate themselves, etc.") in place of 1QS 5, 1: *wzh hsrk l'nšy hyḥd hmtndbym* ("This is the rule for the men of the community who dedicate themselves, etc."). The word *mdrš* appears to mean "an interpretation" (of the Torah) and is used as a title for the section. There is a final occurrence in a MS from 4Q in cryptic script A which preserves on the back of one

---

17. J. T. Milik, "Le travail d'édition des manuscrits de Qumrân," *RB* 63 (1956) 61.

18. "A mi[d]rash of (from?) [m[d]rš m'šry...] Happy is the man that walketh not in the counsel of the wicked. The meaning [pšr] of the passa[ge concerns] those who turn aside from etc." For the text and translations see J. M. Allegro, "Fragments of a Qumran Scroll of Eschatological *Midrāšîm*," *JBL* 77 (1958) 350-54 and Y. Yadin, "A Midrash on 2 Sam vii and Ps i-ii (4Q Florilegium)," *IEJ* 9 (1959) 95-98.

19. Milik, *loc. cit.*

20. J. Carmignac (*La règle de la guerre* [Paris, 1958] 1) proposes that the *lamed* here is a *lamed auctoris*.

fragment (probably of the last column of the work) the title in square letters: *mdrš spr mwšh* ("Interpretation/exposition of the book of Moses"). Again we have an example of *mdrš* used as a title, but unfortunately Milik gives no indication of the nature of the work. [21]

By the time of the QL, then, *midrāš* had clearly come to mean "interpretation," as had also the verb *drš*. [22] We may conclude, because of its varied use and the need to express the object *tôrâ* when referring to biblical endeavors, that the stem does not of itself connote *biblical* interpretation. Also, when it is used in that connection the word seems to have a much more comprehensive meaning than *pērûš*

---

21. Milik, *loc. cit.* F. M. Cross (*The Ancient Library of Qumran and Modern Biblical Studies* [2d ed.; New York, 1961] 46) remarks that the contents of the cryptic documents belong to well-known categories of literature at Qumrân but does not specify further.

22. In QL the verb *drš* occurs 41 times, in eight of the OT meanings ("beseech, seek, promote, take care of, seek out, search, examine and study") as well as in the new meaning "interpret" (in the phrase *dwrš htwrh* in CD 6, 7; 7, 18; 4QFl 1, 11; *dwršy* [*h*]*ḥlqwt* in 1QH 2, 15. 32; 4QpNah 1, 2. 7; 2, 2. 4; 3, 3. 6; 4QpIs^c 10, and *dršw hḥlqwt* in CD 1, 18). In all the occurrences in the meaning "study" and "interpret" (16x) the object has some connection with Scripture (*twrh, mšpt, ḥlqwt*)—40 percent of the total occurrences of the verb as compared on the one hand with two out of 166 in the OT and on the other hand with the widespread use of *drš* in connection with Scripture in the rabbinic literature.—The Greek verb *zēteō*, by which *dāraš* is so often rendered in LXX, never assumed in pre-NT Greek the meaning of interpretation, nor apparently did the nouns *zētēsis* and *zētēma*. However, in some cases where they occur in the NT the nouns seem to be the equivalent of Hebrew *midrāš* (cf. Acts 18, 15; 23, 29; 25, 19; 26, 3; 1 Tm 1, 4 [*exzētēsis*]; 6, 4; 2 Tm 2, 23; Ti 3, 9); cf. Gertner, *art. cit.*, 12-14).

and *pēšer.* [23]   In the use of *mdrš* as a title nothing indicates
that it is employed as a technical term there either.   From
the limited evidence we have it seems to be simply a common
noun.   Its occurrence as a title for a *pēšer* happens to be
on a complex type *pēšer* which utilizes biblical citations on
a secondary level (4QF1),[24] but it is hard to believe that
it was limited to this type of *pēšer* alone.   Certainly its use
was not limited to just the *pešārîm,* for in 4QS *mdrš* is
also applied to what apparently is a codified body of in-
ferences from the Scriptures with some possible dependence
on explicit biblical citations. [25]

THE WORD *Midrāš* IN THE RABBINIC LITERATURE

In the later rabbinic literature [26] the noun *midrāš* retained the meaning "study, inquiry," but its main use was

---

23. *Pērûš* seems to mean "exact interpretation" or a detailed
specification of the Torah precepts, and *pēšer* means allegorical
historization or actualization of dreams/prophecies (see Gertner,
art. cit., 16-18; Silberman, *art. cit.,* 326-35; M. Delcor, "Contribution
à l'étude de la législation des sectaires de Damas et de Qumrân," *RB*
62 [1955] 69-72).

24. Cf. W. R. Lane, "A New Commentary Structure in 4Q
Florilegium," *JBL* 78 (1959) 343-46.

25. Of the three explicit citations of Scripture in 1QS (5, 15.
17; 8, 13-14) two are in col. 5.   It will be interesting to see what
role if any these played in the earlier version.

26. Cf. Gertner, *art. cit.,* 4-14; Bacher, *Terminologie,* I, 25-28,
34-36, 42-43, 103-105, 117-21, 201-202; II, 41-43, 53-56, 107, 119-20,
173; *id.,* "The Origin of the Word Haggadah (Agada)," *JQR* 4
(1892) 406-29; *id.,* "Les trois branches de la science de le vieille
tradition juive," *Revue des études juives* 38 (1899) 211-19; E.
Margulies [Heb. *mrglywt!*], "The Term *drš* in Talmud and Midrash
[Heb.]," *Lešônēnû* 20 (1956) 50-61; I. Heinemann, "The Development of the Terms of Biblical Interpretation [Heb.]," *Lešônēnû* 14
(1946) 182-89.

in the meaning "Scriptural interpretation." In this sense
it designated the procedure, as well as the thing produced:
the single interpretative statement (pl. *midrāšôt*). It also
designated a collection of such interpretations (pl. *midrāšîm*).
Furthermore it was used to desiginate a branch of Jewish
oral tradition. The whole of oral tradition was called Mishnah (in the broad sense) and within Mishnah most rabbis [27]
distinguished three objects and activities of study:

    a) Midrash—the interpretation of the Bible, especially
       legislative portions of the Pentateuch.

    b) Halakah (or Halakoth or Mishnah [in the restricted
       sense])—the systematic and topical assembling of
       halakic (legal) statements extracted from the Midrash
       and presented without their biblical proof-texts.

    c) Haggadah (or Haggadoth)—non-legal biblical inter-
       pretation.

The Midrash, then, was the traditional literature that ar-
ranged the rabbinic material in biblical sequence around
specific texts. It was that literature which was so structured

---

27. Sometimes in an enumeration of all the parts of the oral
tradition the term Haggadah is omitted and the term *midrāš* then
designates haggadic interpretation of Scripture as well as halakic.
Sometimes, also, *midrāš* was used interchangeably with the term
talmûd. *Talmûd* (in the period before it became the name of a
literary work) had for one of its meaning "the exegetical discussion
and proving of halakic statements." In this usage the term *talmûd*
was close to the term *midrāš* in the tripartite division above and was
sometimes used in place of it. *Talmûd* and *midrāš* were not exactly
synonymous, however, and when they were used in opposition to
each other a difference in meaning appeared: *talmûd* starts from
the halakic statement and seeks to find a biblical foundation or
motivation for it, while *midrāš* takes its departure from the biblical
text and argues to a halakic statement (Bacher, *Terminologie*, I,
201).

that it started with a biblical text and then set down in connection with the text edifying thoughts or legislation which the rabbis had drawn out of that text. Midrash in this sense was not so much a technical literary term as a technical theological term based on a literary characteristic, the fact that the works so named were so structured that their discussions took their departure from Scripture and were not structured topically or according to some other plan.

The Babylonian Amoraim apparently were the first to use the Aramaic nouns *pešat* and *dᵉraš* to designate the plain sense of Scripture and free rabbinic interpretation respectively. From then on, the Hebrew and Aramaic nouns *dᵉrāšâ* and *dᵉraš* came to be used more and more frequently to designate this free, homiletic exposition which sought to go more deeply than the plain sense and to draw out the hidden meanings of the Scriptures, and in time even the Hebrew and Aramaic verbs become colored by this usage. In the post-Amoraic period the word *midrāš* also came to designate the *dᵉraš* type of exegesis and was used to set off the earlier homiletic from the later scientific exposition. In this period also, the term haggadah gradually came to include more than non-legal biblical interpretation and designated such things as folklore, sayings of the rabbis, fables, geography, medicine, astronomy, etc. [28] The word haggadah had earlier been used interchangeably with the term midrash (when haggadah had

---

28. Gertner, *art. cit.*, 25-27. *Hamburger Realencyclopädie des Judentums* (Neustrelitz, 1896) II, 19.—From this period on Jewish oral tradition could be divided in two ways, one according to *content* and the other according to *form*. According to *content* the oral tradition falls into halakah (legal) and haggadah (nonlegal) material. The halakah is transmitted in two forms: Midrash in which a text of Scripture is interpreted and the law derived from it is

meant only biblical interpretation), and it is apparently for this reason that occasionally, but not frequently, in this later period the same interchange is still made, so that as a result about one to two percent of the works called midrash have no connection with Scripture but contain merely rabbinic sayings, folklore, etc. [29]

given, or Mishnah which is a codification of laws presented independently of the scriptural bases. The haggadah is either interpretative (presented as exposition of Scripture—midrash) or free (legends, proverbs, etc., having no connection with the Scriptures and presented independently of Scripture). According to *form*, oral tradition falls into Midrash, Mishnah, and free haggadah. The Midrash embraces haggadic and halakic interpretation of the Scriptures. Mishnah is the codification of independent halakic statements. Free haggadah is non-interpretative haggadic material.

29. For example in A. Jellinek, *Bet ha-Midrasch* (2d ed.; Jerusalem, 1938), one finds the Midrash Maase Tora (II, 92-101) and the Midrash Leolam (III, 109-120) which are really collections of sayings of the rabbis. One also finds various forms of the Alphabet Midrash of Rabbi Akiba (III, 12-49; 50-64, etc.), a discussion of the significance and use of each letter of the alphabet. (It is pointed out in the midrash that these letters are the ones God used to write the Scriptures and perhaps that was the reason the work received the title of midrash. It would not be as far-fetched to the rabbinic mentality as it would be to ours.) There are also assorted versions of the deuterocanonical book of Judith. Some are simply entitled *The Story of Judith* (I, 130-31; II, 12-22) but others are entitled *Midrash for Hanukkah* (I, 132-36). The reason for the title midrash is not clear. Perhaps it is simply an example of midrash being used to designate free haggadah. Perhaps it was felt that the reworking of a revered but non-canonical work of antiquity could be called a midrash as well as the reworking of a biblical text. Perhaps its use as a homily (normally being on the Bible and therefore a midrash) for the feast of Hanukkah was the influencing factor.—For the rarity of midrash as a title for non-exegetical works see B. Heller, "Agadische Literatur," *Encyclopaedia Judaica* I (Berlin, 1928) 979-1036; Strack, *op. cit.* (see Introduction, n. 21).

MODERN USAGE

The term midrash is used by the Jews in modern Hebrew, and in other languages as a loan word, in the same manner as the word was used in the rabbinic material.

Among biblical scholars today the term midrash has become a technical literary term to designate a literary genre. This is a modern usage of the word and is based on the *rabbinic* term *midrāš*. The word is employed to designate that type of literature called midrash by the rabbis as well as other material judged to manifest the same characteristics. However, as was pointed out in the introduction, there is not much agreement among exegetes on what exactly is called midrash by the rabbis or on the characteristics of midrash; and another reason why this is so is now evident: the Jews themselves have not always been precise in their own use of the term.   The word midrash is also used modernly by scholars to designate the *dᵉraš* type of exegesis.

CONCLUSIONS

At this point the following conclusions may be drawn:

1) When the term midrash is used among biblical scholars today as a name for a *literary genre,* the implication in this *literary* usage is that the word is based, not on the rabbinic usage of *midrāš* to designate the *activity* of study or the *activity* of biblical interpretation or a *type of exegesis,* but on that rabbinic usage which designates a specific *corpus of literature* within Jewish oral tradition.   This distinction has not always been borne in mind in recent discussions of the literary form, the word midrash being

used within the same discussion to designate biblical study and a type of exegesis as well as a literary classification, as if all were synonymous. And clearly all are not synonymous. There is exegesis of the *d^eraš* type in the Talmud and yet the Talmud is not called a midrash by the rabbis; and the study of the Bible (midrash) produced all three branches of oral tradition, yet all are not called midrash.

2) In the case of the genre midrash, most of the early works that gave rise to the tradition are not extant, so we are unable to study the genre by way of its historical development. In fact, the bulk of the extant material of the tradition is found in the rabbinic literature of the common era and represents the final stages of the literary tradition. Consequently in building up the modern classification, critics have set up as the exemplar that corpus of literature designated by the rabbis as midrash and then have worked back from there, including in the same category any earlier works that manifest the same characteristics. The method is sound in view of the circumstances, provided that we do not view the rabbinic midrash as a fixed goal toward which the earlier authors had been tending, and see it almost as a Platonic archetype, the pure idea of the genre, of which a writer has a vision, toward which he strives but at which he never wholly arrives. [30] In building up the classification in this manner it will of course be necessary to analyze the rabbinic midrashic literature and to describe its characteristics to provide a basis for grouping other works with it, but we cannot expect all of these characteristics to

30. Neo-classicism is generally blamed for this error. See Ehrenpreis, *op. cit.*, 7-8.

be found in the earlier works in the tradition. We must distinguish between characteristics constitutive of the form (primary) and the ones that are incidental or acquired in the process of development (secondary). And even in stating the primary characteristics, we must not think that we are thereby describing some sort of heavenly pattern of the genre. Rather we are attempting to provide the basis for recovering the historical development of a tradition of literature in a situation where we must work from the later examples to the earlier. And when we speak of the rabbinic midrash as the exemplar of the genre, we do so only from the point of view of our modern attempts at classification and not from the point of view of the original authors.

3) What is the extent of this corpus of rabbinic literature that is the exemplar and which must be analyzed for its primary characteristics? Is it just the material dealing with the Scriptures, or is it also the folklore, etc., of the later haggadah, since an occasional work of this sort is entitled midrash? Folklore, fables, etc., which have no connection with the Bible or are not used in connection with biblical interpretation were regularly called haggadah (modernly: free haggadah in opposition to interpretative haggadah or midrash). Only in a few cases do we find the word midrash applied to such non-exegetical material and it seems legitimate to conclude that this late rabbinic usage is an improper one, occasioned by the gradual broadening of the term haggadah with which midrash had once been interchangeable. Our modern technical term midrash is a term that is intended to be precise and its meaning should therefore be confined to the *proper* meaning of the rabbinic term, and midrash when properly used by the rabbis designated

works dealing with Scripture. [31]   The exemplar, therefore, for our modern literary category is that literature which falls under this proper rabbinic meaning.

4) Some works written prior to the rabbinic material bear the title "midrash" (in Chr and the QL), but one cannot automatically apply to them the modern technical term midrash solely on that account.   As best we can tell at the moment from the small number of occurrences extant, the pre-rabbinic word midrash seems to be nothing more than a generic term with a variety of meanings and has not yet taken on the technical meaning found later among the rabbis.   If we are to include pre-rabbinic literary pieces under our modern category of midrash, we should do so only on the grounds that they possess the *primary characteristics* of midrash as found in the rabbinic works.

---

31. This is clear not only in its use as a title but also in those texts where the word *midrāš* is used by the rabbis with some precision. When the word *midrāš* is deliberately contrasted with another word, it very clearly means that traditional literature whose structure is such that it explicitly or implicitly starts with a text of Scripture and comments on it.   *Midrāš* means this when it is used in opposition to *talmûd* (see n. 27 above) and also when it is set off against the word Halakah (Halakoth), e.g., in the triple division Midrash, Halakoth, Haggadot.

Chapter 3
The Characteristics of Rabbinic Midrash

A distinctive characteristic of postexilic Judaism was the great importance accorded to the Torah. This was not the introduction of a new element into Israel's faith, but a new emphasis, a greater stress on a feature that had always been of central importance. The exile had naturally resulted in a heightened interest in the Torah. The Torah was the only sacred possession which was left to the Jews in Babylon, nation and cult having vanished. Furthermore, the prophets had explained the calamity of the exile as a penalty for sinning against Yahweh's Law and it is not at all surprising that the Jews felt that the future must be marked by a greater fidelity to the Law's demands. And thus, after the return from the exile and especially from the time of Ezra's reform, the Law actually became the organizing principle of the community of the restoration. Moreover, very soon after the return, the living prophetic word had ceased, and thenceforth if anyone was to seek God, inquire of God, determine His will, he must of necessity seek in the Torah.

This emphasis on the Torah led to the final redaction of the Pentateuch, and this literary activity created in the succeeding centuries a favorable milieu for the final redaction, composition, and canonization of the remaining books of the OT and for the gradual fixing of the text.

Partly as a result of the exaltation of the Torah and the emergence of a more or less fixed text of the Pentateuch, partly because of the inaccessability of the Temple worship to all, there was gradually introduced into Jewish life the public reading and teaching of the Torah (and later of the Prophets and Writings as well). This new form of public worship existed alongside of the Temple cult and by the Hellenistic era had developed into the synagogue service properly speaking. When the teachers began to read and teach the Torah to the people there was immediately revealed the rift between life as found in the Pentateuch and life as it was lived. Life is always ahead of the written law, there being added in the course of time many different customs, practices, and precepts to meet the needs of a developed and extended society and to specify general laws. And thus there was found the need for interpretation of the legal portions of the Torah to bridge the gap between past and present by justifying existing practices and by developing new laws or new interpretations of old laws (halakah). Likewise the nonlegal portions of the Torah and the rest of the Scriptures required interpretation for they had become the primary source of ethical and inspirational teaching; and just as the full meaning and correct application of the legal material of the Torah was searched out, so also the full meaning of the historical records and of the prophecies and the ethical lessons to be derived from the stories of the fathers were drawn out of the Scriptures and applied to the needs of the present (haggadah). And with the destruction of the

Temple and the intensifying of persecution an increased demand was made upon the haggadah—namely to supply comfort to the downtrodden and inspire them with hope.

This interpretative activity, first mentioned in connection with Ezra's memorable convocation (Neh 8, 7-8) and continued by the teachers of subsequent generations, resulted in an accumulation of a body of traditional legislation as well as explanations and comments on the written Scriptures. Oral at first, this material was later collected and committed to writing. Laws were codified according to subject, generally independently of their Scriptural backing, in collections such as the Mishnah of Rabbi Judah; the interpretative material was compiled in other works among which are those collections of the second to the thirteenth century after Christ that are known as the midrashim. [1] By the end of the fifth century (or according to a more recent view, the end of the second century [2]) creative interpretative activity had virtually ceased. Thereafter the tendency was toward elaboration, codification, and compilation until the thirteenth century when, after a gradual process, the midrash was completely superseded by the more modern sciences: history, theology, grammatical exposition, and the counterpart of science, Kabalah.

---

1. Lists of the extant midrashim with a description of their contents, approximate dates of composition and redactions, printed editions and translations, etc., can be found in Strack, *op. cit.*; *The Jewish Encyclopedia*, arts. "Midrash Haggadah," "Midrash Halakah," "Midrashim, Smaller"; *Encyclopaedia Judaica*, art. "Agadische Literatur." More recent translations not mentioned there include H. Freedman and M. Simon, eds.; *Midrash Rabbah*, 9 vols. (London: Soncino Press, 1951); J. Lauterbach, *Mekilta de-Rabbi Ishmael*, 3 vols. (Philadelphia, 1933-35); W. Braude, *The Midrash on Psalms*, 2 vols. (New Haven, 1959).

2. Vermes, *op. cit.* (see Introduction, n. 19), 228-29.

The primitive *Sitz im Leben,* therefore, of the halakah was the discussions of the rabbinical schools, and the *Sitz im Leben* of the haggadah (and of the popular halakah) was the preaching which followed the biblical reading in the cultic assemblies on Sabbaths and festivals, and the preaching on important public and private occasions (war, famine, circumcision, weddings, funerals, etc.). The midrashim, which, as we have already said, are compilation works, are therefore collections of material culled directly or indirectly from these sources, and in discussing the general structure of the midrashim we must always remember that we are dealing with artificial structures.

THE LITERARY STRUCTURE OF THE MIDRASHIM

From the point of view of literary structure, the midrashim can be classified under three headings: (1) exegetical midrashim; (2) homiletic midrashim; (3) and narrative midrashim.

1) *Exegetical Midrashim*: When the rabbis undertook to edit, revise, and collect the immense body of exegetical material, one form that suggested itself was to arrange individual interpretations in textual sequence and thus to construct a verse-by-verse exposition of the individual books of the Bible (although in many cases all the verses are not provided with interpretation, especially in the latter chapters of books and in the Psalms). Various long and short explanations of successive passages were strung together and to this running commentary were added at times longer disquisitions and narratives connected in some way with the verse in question or with one of the explanations. Often in these interpretations references are made to other scriptural passages and the text being commented upon is

considered in the light of these other citations. There are
also references to circumstances and historical events contemporary with the original interpreter—it being characteristic
of the midrash to view the personages and conditions of
the Bible in the light of contemporary history. We cite
a few examples from *Bereshith Rabbah* and *Midrash Tehillim*: [3]

AND IT CAME TO PASS, AS THEY JOURNEYED
FROM THE EAST (*MIKKEDEM*) (Gn 11, 2). They
travelled from further east to nearer east. R. Leazar b.
R. Simeon interpreted: They betook themselves away
from the Ancient (*kadmon*) of the world, saying, "We
refuse to accept either Him or His Divinity."
THAT THEY FOUND A PLAIN. R. Judah said:
All the nations of the world assembled to discover which
plain would hold them all, and eventually they found
it. R. Nehemiah observed: THEY FOUND: thus it is
written, *If it concerneth the scorners, He permits them
to scorn* (Jb 3, 34).
AND THEY DWELT THERE. R. Isaac said: Wherever you find dwelling mentioned, Satan becomes active.
R. Helbo said: Wherever you find contentment, Satan
brings accusations. R. Levi said: Wherever you find
eating and drinking, the arch-robber [Satan] cuts his
capers [is up to mischief].
AND THEY SAID TO ONE ANOTHER (Gn 11, 3).
Who said to whom? Said R. Berekiah: Mizraim said to
Cush.
COME, LET US MAKE BRICKS, AND BURN THEM
(*WE-NISREFAH*) THOROUGHLY: This is written

---

3. The translations are from Freedman and Simon, *op. cit.*, and
Braude, *op. cit.*

wenissorfah (and we will be burnt): this people is destined to be burnt out of the world.

AND THEY HAD BRICK FOR STONE, etc. R. Huna said: Their work prospered: a man came to lay one [stone] and he laid two; he came to plaster one [row] and plastered two.

AND THEY SAID: COME LET US BUILD A CITY, AND A TOWER (Gn 11, 4). R. Judan said: The tower they built, but they did not build the city. An objection is raised: But it is written, *And the Lord came down to see the city and the tower* (*ib.* 5)? Read what follows, he replied: *And they left off to build the city* (*ib.* 8), the tower, however, not being mentioned. R. Hiyya b. Abba said: A third of this tower which they built sank [into the earth], a third was burnt, while a third is still standing. And should you think that it [the remaining third] is small—R. Huna said in R. Idi's name: When one ascends to the top, he sees the palm trees below him like grasshoppers. (*Bereshith Rabbah* 38, 7-8).

I WILL MAKE HIM A HELP (*'EZER*) AGAINST HIM (*KE-NEGDO*) (Gn. 2, 8): if he is fortunate, she is a help; if not she is against him. R. Joshua b. Nehemiah said: If a man is fortunate, she is like the wife of Hananiah b. Hakinai; if not, she is like the wife of R. Jose the Galilean. R. Jose the Galilean had a bad wife; she was his sister's daughter, and used to put him to shame. His disciples said to him: "Master, divorce this woman, for she does not act as benefits your honour." "Her dowry is too great for me, and I cannot afford to divorce her," was his reply. Now it happened once that he and R. Eleazar b. 'Azariah were sitting and studying, and when they finished, the latter

asked him, "Sir, will you kindly permit that we go to
your home together?" "Yes," replied he. As they
entered, she cast down her gaze [in anger] and was
making her way out, when he looked at a pot standing
on the pot-range and asked her, "Is there anything in
the pot?" "There's a hash in it," she answered. He
went and uncovered it, and found in it some chickens.
Now R. Eleazar b. 'Azariah knew what he had heard,
and as they sat together and were eating he observed,
"Sir, did she not say it was hash, yet we have found
chickens?" "A miracle has happened," replied he.
When they finished he said to him: "Master, abandon
this woman, for she does not treat you with proper respect." "Sir," he replied, "her dowry is too great for
me and I cannot divorce her." "We [your pupils],"
said the other, "will apportion her dowry among ourselves, so you can divorce her." And they did so, etc.
etc. (*Bereshith Rabbah* 17, 3)

[A PSALM] OF DAVID. UNTO THEE, O LORD,
DO I LIFT UP MY SOUL (Ps 25, 1). These words
are to be considered in the light of the verse *In the
same day thou shalt give him his hire, neither shall the
sun go down upon it; for he is poor, and he lifteth his
soul unto him* (Dt 24, 15). The Holy One, blessed be
He, asked David: "David, why dost thou lift up thy
soul unto Me?" David replied: Because upon Thine
earth I am a hireling before Thee: *A servant that
eagerly longeth for the shadow, and . . . a hireling that
looketh for the reward of his work* (Jb 7, 2). And it
is written of a hireling in the Law of Moses *In the same
day thou shalt give him his hire.* And so *Unto Thee,
O Lord, do I lift up my soul.* For in the world's use

the hireling who completes his work for a householder asks the householder for the wage of his work, and the householder gives it to him. And shall it not be so with the Holy One, blessed be He? Shall not the words *neither shall the sun go down upon [a man's hire]* apply also to the Holy One, blessed be He? Now if it is said of a hireling who asks the wage which the householder owes him, *He lifteth his soul unto him,* how much more ought this be said of us whose lives depend on Thee! (*Midrash Tehillim* 25, 1)

The Tannaitic midrashim (generally classified as halakic but containing haggadic material as well: *Mekilta, Sifre, Sifra,* etc.) follow this exegetical form throughout. However, many of the later haggadic midrashim differ in this that the several "parashiyyot" (sections, chapters) are introduced by proems such as characterize the beginnings of homilies. Thus they are a combination of running commentary and homily. There are also minor haggadic works that use the exegetical format but treat of selected passages of Scripture rather than of entire books of the Bible. There are even some midrashic works that are completely folklore, tales of the rabbis, etc., but they take their departure from a single biblical text and thus present the material in such a way that it is in the service of the Bible; e.g., the Midrash *'Elle Ezkerah* which describes the execution of ten noted Tannaim but in connection with Ps 42, 5.

In none of these exegetical compilations was an attempt made to reproduce in full the contents of the original sermons. The midrashim merely record in an abbreviated form the central ideas from which flowed the whole process of thought of the preachers and around which they wove their homilies. This accounts for the style of these collections being laconic, pithy, and terse at times to the point of obscurity, so that the reader feels that he is faced with a kind of super-shorthand. As William Braude has remarked, "the world of Midrash may thus be described as a garden of dried flowers. And at times only a combination of love, reverence, and learning can breathe life into leaves and blossoms which to a hasty and unsympathetic eye appear to be dead." [4]

2) *Homiletic Midrashim*: Not all of the midrashic works arrange the haggadic material in textual sequence. Some of the compilations—the homiletic midrashim—present the traditional interpretative material in the form of homilies. The homiletic midrashim, therefore, contain more extended discussions of texts than do the exegetical midrashim, but on the other hand they present exegetical material only for selected verses of the Bible, usually the verses that form the beginning of the Scripture readings in the synagogues. [5]

Bacher defended the position that the homiletic midrashim contain hardly any authentic homilies but are rather a collection of proems to homilies. [6]   Others like Philipp Bloch think that actual homilies are preserved in these midrashim. [7]   Recent study seems to indicate that both

---

4. Braude, *op. cit.*, I, xx.

5. The Scripture readings are either Pentateuchal pericopes according to the triennial Palestinian cycle which divides the Pentateuch into 154-175 Sedarim, or Pentateuchal and prophetic pericopes according to the Pesikta cycle for festivals and special Sabbaths. Both "Sedarim" and "Pesikta" homilies are found in the extant midrashim.

6. W. Bacher, *Die Proömien der alten jüdischen Homilie* (Leipzig, 1913) 1-4.

7. Ph. Bloch, "Studien zur Aggadah," *MGWJ* 34 (1885) 174-84, 210-24, 257-64.

of these viewpoints are inadequate, that real sermons are not preserved in these midrashim, but that the structures or patterns used in the real homilies have been employed in a rather mechanical way to collect the units of traditional material within them and form artificial homilies.[8] Many of these homiletic patterns have been described,[9] but a discussion of these would take us beyond the scope of this book where we are concerned simply with the genre's primary characteristics or gross qualifications. However, attention to these sub-traditions within the genre would be necessary if one is to classify a given work with precision and certainty; and studies of this nature such as those of Silberman[10] and Borgen[11] show that this literary labor can be exegetically rewarding as well.

3) *Narrative Midrashim*: These works exemplify what Geza Vermes has called the "rewritten Bible" type of midrash: a completely rewritten biblical narrative embellished

---

8. P. Borgen, *Bread From Heaven* (Leiden, 1965) 56-57. Cf. the similar viewpoint of Zunz, *op. cit.* (see Introd., n. 21), 359-60.

9. J. Theodor, "Zur Composition der agadischen Homilien," *MGWJ* 28 (1879) 97-113, 164-75, 271-78, 337-50, 408-18, 455-62; 29 (1880) 19-23; Ph. Bloch, "Studien zur Aggadah," *MGWJ* 34 (1885) 166-84, 210-24, 257-69, 385-404; 35 (1886) 165-87, 389-405; S. Maybaum, *Die ältesten Phasen in der Entwicklung der jüdischen Predigt* (Berlin, 1901); W. Bacher, *Die Proömien:...;* A. Marmorstein, "The Background of the Haggadah," *HUCA* 6 (1929) 141-204; E. Stein, "Die homiletische Peroratio im Midrasch," *HUCA* 8-9 (1931-32) 353-71; J. Mann, *The Bible as Read and Preached in the Old Synagogue*, I (Cincinnati, 1940); M. Smith, *Tannaitic Parallels to the Gospels* (*JBL* Monograph Series VI; Philadelphia, 1951) 101-109; H. Thyen, *Der Stil der jüdisch-hellenistischen Homilie* (Göttingen, 1955).

10. Silberman, *art. cit.* (see Introd., n. 4), on the Qumrân *pēšer*.

11. Borgen, *op. cit.*, on Jn 6.

with legends and non-biblical traditions (e.g., *Sefer ha-yashar, Pirke de-Eleazar, Midrash Wayyissa'u, Dibre ha-yamim shel Mosheh, Midrash Wayyosha', Midrash Petirath 'Aharon, Midrash Petirath Moshe,* etc). In this type the interpretative material is not given at the side of the Scripture text, as it were, but is worked right into the biblical text to form a continuous narrative. [12]

THE PURPOSE AND TECHNIQUES OF THE LITERATURE

The purpose of the midrashic literature was to make the Bible relevant and meaningful, to interpret it and draw out from it all of the lessons contained therein. The exegesis that we find in the midrashim is of a twofold character. There is first of all a considerable amount of literal exegesis (exposition of the *peshat* or plain meaning) which shows evidence of fine linguistic sense, good judgment, and acute insight into the biblical text. [13]   But side by side with this there is an even larger mass of expositions far removed from the actual meaning of the text (*deraš* interpretations): biblical accounts are embellished with fanciful details; many things are drawn out of the Bible which the original authors clearly never intended; the biblical text is even altered in many daring ways and apparently without hesitation.

The methods used for the exposition of the *peshat* we need not dwell upon here. They are in many ways the same as the techniques of our own day (based on grammar, lexicography, critical analysis of the text) and while they are

---

12. See, for example, Vermes' discussion of *Sefer ha-Yashar* in *Scripture and Tradition in Judaism,* 67-95.

13. Cf. I. Frankel, *Peshat in Talmudic and Midrashic Literature* (Toronto, 1956); Braude, *op. cit.,* I, xvi-xvii.

not identical with modern techniques they can be understood on the basis of our own biblical research. Requiring some comment are the methods employed for the $d^e ra\check{s}$ exegesis. Isaac Heinemann in his study of the methods of the haggadah [14] divides the $d^e ra\check{s}$ methods into two general categories: creative historiography and creative philogy; [15] and this provides a convenient schema for our treatment here.

Creative historiography is the complementing and amplification of the available facts in an imaginative manner. The method is found in all three forms of rabbinic midrash—the only difference being that in the narrative midrashim the amplifications are worked in with the original data to form a new running account, while in the exegetical and homiletic midrashim the embellishing of history remains external to the original text and is done in the form of outside "data" brought to the text for exegetical purposes. Creative historiography is, of course, not peculiar to midrash. It is found in free haggadah (Jewish folk literature) and in popular history, as well as in the folk literature and popular history of other nations where its use has a variety of motives underlying it. [16] In midrash its use is an exegetical and homiletic one primarily, its purpose being to clarify the Scriptures and to make the biblical text relevant in one way or another for the writer's audience. Thus, embellishments are used to clarify stories and to answer questions raised by lacunae in

---

14. I. Heinemann, *Darkê ha-Aggadah* (2d ed.; Jerusalem, 1954). For a summary and review of the book see *Jewish Social Studies* 13 (1951) 181-84, and J. Bonsirven, "Interpretatio Aggadica," *VD* 30 (1952) 349-52.

15. In his choice of terms Heinemann is influenced by subjective idealism (cf. *op. cit.*, 4-11). We retain the terms here without subscribing to the philosophical presuppositions.

16. Heinemann, *op. cit.*, 1, 24, 27-28, 35, 39, 44-46.

the text, to aid in the understanding of the text, to eliminate historical and doctrinal problems raised by the Bible itself, and to satisfy curiosity. As a homiletic technique amplifications on the text serve to illustrate abstract truths which one wishes to join to the text or which are suggested by the text. They are means of imparting instruction and inspiration. They make the biblical narrative more attractive, more contemporary, more edifying, more intelligible, and, by filling out many of the briefly mentioned and shadowy figures of the Bible, they make the narrative much more real. [17]   This is not to say, however, that exegetical and homiletic motives were the only ones operative. Some of the embellishments in the midrashim were also prompted by the motivation behind any folk literature—the desire to tell a good story—for, undoubtedly, in the course of exegeting and moralizing, the midrashist warmed to his task and elaborated to some degree merely for the sake of elaboration and out of a delight for imaginative details. [18]   But this was not the primary purpose. It might be helpful here to cite Marc Connelly's *Green Pastures* [19] as a non-rabbinic parallel to illustrate, *servatis servandis,* something of the process and mentality involved and to provide a basis for sympathetic understanding of the rabbinic counterparts.

The term *creative philology* would cover all of those techniques of the rabbis whereby they made deductions from the Scriptures and drew out hidden meanings. In the case of creative historiography it is almost impossible to give methodological formulae from the rabbis themselves. The permission to *develop and expand* the biblical material

---

17. *Ibid.,* 21-25, 27-29, 34-37, 56-57, 60, etc.
18. *Ibid.,* 23, 49, etc.
19. New York, 1929.

seems to have been self-evident.   The situation appears to
be somewhat different concerning *deduction* from the biblical text, for here the rabbis actually formed certain exegetical rules by which the Torah was to be interpreted. [20]
However, these rules are primarily concerned with halakah
and were looked upon as merely a helpful guide for the
haggadist, and so are not an exhaustive list of the rabbinic
techniques.   Two general principles, however, governed the
rabbis' approach to the text of Scripture. [21]   (1) *One must
interpret all the minute details in Scripture.*   This principle
was based to some extent on the conviction that the Torah
is a divine book and that it does not speak in human language.   Unlike the language of men, God's word has many
meanings for he can say many things at once.   Hence in
this divine language everything is significant and is there
to impart knowledge: e.g., anything superfluous in the text,
any omissions, the order in which things are referred to,
any deviations from common language and spelling, etc.
(2) *All parts of the Bible* (the letters, the words, the verses,
and the sections) *may be explained not only as a continuity
in relation to the contex*t (as with human documents), *but*

---

20. Cf. Strack, *op. cit.* (see Introd., n. 21), 93-98. On this aspect
of rabbinic interpretation, in addition to the work of Heinemann cited,
see also I. Heinemann, *Altjüdische Allegoristik* (Breslau, 1936);
J. Bonsirven, *Exégèse rabbinique et exégèse paulinienne* (Paris, 1938)
1-259; D. Daube, "Rabbinic Methods of Interpretation and Hellenistic Rhetoric," *HUCA* 22 (1949) 239-64; *id.*, "Alexandrian Methods
of Interpretation and the Rabbis," *Fest. Hans Lewald* (Basel, 1953)
27-44; A. Kaminka, "Bibel VII, Bibel-exegese," *Encyclopaedia Judaica*, IV (Berlin, 1929) 619-28; S. Lieberman, *Hellenism in Jewish
Palestine* (New York, 1950) 47-82; J. Weingreen, "The Rabbinic
Approach to the Study of the Old Testament," *BJRylL* 34 (1951-52)
166-90; M. Kadushin, *The Rabbinic Mind* (New York, 1952) 1-142.

21. Heinemann, *Aggadah,* 96-107.

also as autonomous units, for the parts retain an independent significance as well as unlimited possibilities of combination with each other. Thus we find the letters of words being scrutinized for meaning through their numerical values, being made into acrostics, rearranged to form other words, etc. We find the words of sentences being rearranged, revocalized, assigned alternate meanings; and we find sections being interpreted allegorically, being connected with unrelated sections in other parts of the Bible, etc.

The existence of large quantities of *d^eraš* exegesis in the midrashim as well as the multiple and contradictory interpretations often given to a single text pose the question of how the rabbis could have departed so drastically from the obvious meaning of the text. The question is an old one—discussed even by Maimonides. [22] Modern writers in discussing the problem have rightly called attention to the rabbinic conviction mentioned above that God's word can and does express at once many different things and thus every word and every verse has "49 (or 70) aspects" (*Bemidbar Rabbah* 2, 3; 13, 15-16) or hidden meanings and the exegete can draw out all these meanings over and above the plain sense if only he knows how to do it. It is like striking sparks out of a rock (*Sanhedrin* 34 a-b). However, some of these recent writers have seized upon this belief and have made it more or less the basis of their explanations of the biblical interpretation of rabbinic Judaism. [23] The belief in hidden meanings is indeed a part of the explanation of the *d^eraš* exegesis, and an important part, but not a premise upon which one can construct a whole theory of interpretation, for it tends to

---

22. *Moreh Nebukim* 3, 43.

23. E.g., S. Horovitz, "Midrash," *The Jewish Encyclopedia* 8 (New York, 1904) 548; Lauterbach, *op. cit.* (see n. 1 above), I, xv.

put the hidden meanings on a par with the plain sense and this is something that the rabbis did not do. [24]

It would seem that the true explanation of this dual phenomenon of *peshat* and *deraš* exegesis in the midrashim is to be sought primarily in the homiletic and religious pre-occupations of the interpreters. [25] The purpose of the midrash was the instruction and edification of the masses, and consequently the midrashist by reason of this religious rather than purely scholarly aim endeavored not so much to seek the original meaning of the text as to find religious edification, moral instruction, and sustenance for the thoughts and feelings of his audience. The text of Scripture was the point of departure for it was God's word, valid for all time. The interpreter would begin with the plain sense. If it was useful religiously, it would be thus expounded. But if in the course of his reflection the biblical text suggested some idea other than that immediately apparent, then this idea would be set forth in connection with the text. If the plain sense contained a difficulty and thus an obstacle between the text and the audience, the difficulty would be

---

24. Witness the sober tone of the exegesis in the Mishnah (see S. Rosenblatt, *The Interpretation of the Bible in the Mishnah* [Baltimore, 1935]). Furthermore, the rabbis taught that "a biblical verse never loses its literal meaning" regardless of how the verse may be employed in rabbinic interpretation. This principle affirms that the literal meaning is stable and primary, that rabbinic inter-pretations are added matters and secondary, and that each interpreter should bear in mind the literal meaning of the verse regardless of what his predecessors have done with it.—On this whole question see Heinemann, *Aggadah* 129-30, 136, 153-56; and especially Kadushin, *op. cit.*, 131-42.

25. See Weingreen, *art. cit.* (see n. 20) 173-74, 190; Kadushin, *op. cit.* (see n. 20) 98-121; Heinemann, *Aggadah, passim;* Zunz, *op. cit.* (see Introduction, n. 21) 337-38; *et al.*

solved and, if possible, some religious value also derived. If the plain sense was obvious or if it was not useful religiously, then a hidden meaning would be sought. Throughout the whole process the belief in hidden meanings was not the primary motivating principle, however. It seems to have been a secondary consideration that helped the process along and served to justify the whole activity. The primary aim was to make the Bible relevant, to make the Bible come alive and serve as a source of spiritual nourishment, refreshment and stimulation.

It is sometimes said that the interpretations in the midrashim are in reality attempts by the rabbis to justify or confirm their concepts, ideas, and teachings and to find for them a biblical foundation. Occasionally this is the situation, but it is not the general rule by any means, and to make it such would be to do the rabbis a grave injustice. Actually the biblical texts played a rôle in the development of rabbinic ideas and were not employed simply as pegs for ideas that had already been thought out—and midrashic statements were precisely what they claimed to be: interpretations of the biblical text. We can best describe this interplay between Bible and midrash as one in which the Bible acts as a stimulus for homiletic material, and in this connection there is a certain kinship between midrash and poetry. [26] Both the poem and the midrash are touched off by a stimulus. In poetry it is an object perceived; in midrash it is usually the plain sense of the biblical text. In both cases the stimulus is non-determining: it can produce a multiplicity of effects, for, once the stimulus functions, the poet and the midrashist develop the ensuing thoughts in their own personal and individual ways. Thus it is possible to have

---

26. See especially Kadushin, *op. cit.*, 113-21, 132ff.

many poems on the same object and many interpretations on the same verse. And neither a poem nor a midrash is an integral part of a system of thought, an idea logically inferred from other ideas. On the contrary, both are discrete and individual entities.

Just as with the poem, so also with the midrash, the stimulus may play a more extensive role in the development of the thought than that of a mere initial impetus. The resulting ideas may be more or less cast in the terms of the stimulus and thus the ideas are concretized and their development in some way controlled. Sometimes, however, the ensuing ideas may be quite different from the stimulus. In any case both the poet and the midrashist are obliged to give the "sequence of thought" to show the connection between the stimulus and its effect. Often in the case of midrash the connection with the original text consists of hardly more than a play on words but this verbal connection would be quite sufficient.

Here, of course, the analogy between midrash and poetry ceases. It is the nature of poetry to communicate aesthetic experience, while the midrash is concerned with religious and ethical values, and the thought touched off by the biblical verse is not intended to be judged by standards of style, beauty, and form. But the analogy does help us to see the midrashic comments in their proper relation to the biblical texts and also to account for the multiple and contradictory interpretations often given to a single text.

CONCLUSIONS: THE PRIMARY CHARACTERISTICS
OF RABBINIC MIDRASH

From this brief description of the literary structure, content, methods and aims of the rabbinic midrash, we are now in a position to attempt a statement of the primary characteristics of the literature.

1) *Literary structure*: From the point of view of structure there are several diverse forms of literature that are designated as midrash. There are the exegetical, homiletic and narrative midrashim. Presumably the original synagogue homilies which gave rise to so much of this material were looked upon as a form of midrash too. Moreover, as we pointed out above, every midrashic statement is a logically independent unit that is complete in itself—even to the extent that contradictory interpretations can be placed side by side in the midrashim. The various collection forms (the exegetical and homiletic midrashim as well as the homilies themselves) are merely attempts to unify otherwise independent units so as to make for sustained interest on the part of the audience. Hence an individual midrashic statement can be and was called a midrash also.

A primary characteristic of a genre should be able to be verified in all the manifestations of that genre, and characteristics that are found only in one or another type should be classified as secondary characteristics. We would conclude, therefore, that the basic midrashic structure, common to all forms that can be labeled midrash down to the smallest independent unit, is merely that one begins with a text of Scripture and proceeds to comment on it in some way. The midrashic unit must be so structured that the material contained therein is placed in the context of a Scripture text, and is presented for the sake of the biblical text. Midrash, then, is a literature about a literature.

2) *Aim*: The aim of midrash is to comment on the Scriptures, to make them religiously relevant to the contemporaries of the interpreter, to make yesterday's text

(which is the word of God for all time) meaningful and nourishing for today.   Midrash has primarily, therefore, a religious and edifying aim and not a speculative one.

3) *Content*: Content is the basis for the distinction between halakic and haggadic midrash (legal vs. nonlegal discussion of a text), and therefore content enters into a definition of these two species of midrash.   However, content does not appear to be a factor in the definition of the genre midrash, for there seem to be no topics or themes that are peculiar to midrash or that flow from the very nature of the literature.   We can find in the midrashim discussions of everything from cabbages to kings—literally—and it is very risky to say that a particular theme or topic is not represented in the literature. [27]   And for the same reason no aspects of content other than "legal" and "nonlegal" should enter into the definition of the species halakic and haggadic.

4) *Type of Exegesis*: Is $d^e ra\check{s}$ or creative exegesis among the primary characteristics of the literary form midrash? [28] The question is not easy to answer.   On the one hand it would seem that $d^e ra\check{s}$ exegesis is not among the primary characteristics.   It is true that the rabbinic midrashim con-

---

27. E.g., Lane's claim ("A New Commentary Structure in 4Q Florilegium," *JBL* 78 [1959] 346) that messianic and eschatological orientations are lacking in rabbinic midrash cannot be supported (cf. the conclusions of the homilies).   Nor can Silberman's statement (*art. cit.*, p. 329) that contemporizing is lacking in rabbinic midrash be supported.   For example, the identifications of Edom with Rome, so frequent in the midrashim (and cited by Silberman—p. 331), were contemporizing comments at the time the particular interpretations were composed.

28. $D^e ra\check{s}$ exegesis is of course essential to midrash when the word midrash designates a *type of exegesis*.   Here we speak of midrash in the sense of a literary genre.

tain a vast amount of non-literal exegesis and that as time went on more and more of it was employed in them, but there is also a substantial amount of literal exegesis. It is also true that to a certain extent $d^e ra\check{s}$ exegesis flows from the nature of midrash (in so far as midrash is a popular and devotional type literature and therefore prone to this type of exegesis). But to some extent the $d^e ra\check{s}$ exegesis is due to the concept of Scriptural inspiration in antiquity, i.e., that when God speaks in human language He says hundreds of things at once and thus there are many hidden meanings to be uncovered, and for this reason the $d^e ra\check{s}$ type of exegesis is seemingly an accidental characteristic due to time of composition and other circumstances.

On the other hand there is one fact that suggests that "creative exegesis" is one of the primary characteristics. The production of midrashic literature is commonly thought of as ceasing around the 13th century after Christ with the last of the great compilations, and the word midrash is not used today to describe any modern homiletic exposition of Scripture. Hence the word midrash is by convention reserved for the earlier predominantly creative exegetical literature, and it seems legitimate to conclude that creative exegesis is so frequent and prevalent in the genre that it has become a constitutive element.

For our study the point has little practical importance since the authors of the pre-rabbinic literature in which we shall seek examples of midrash shared the creative exegetical mentality with the later rabbis. The point is of practical importance only if one is seeking to incorporate post-13th century works in the classification, in which case, because of conventional usage, the note of "predominantly creative exegesis" must be expressly stated as a primary characteristic. We should note, however, that in the case of both

pre-rabbinic and post-13th century midrash it is a matter
of *predominantly* creative exegesis; any single midrashic
statement could be of the literal or *p^eshat* type.

5) *Exegetical Methods*: The techniques of exegesis
found in rabbinic midrash are not among the primary characteristics of the literary form, and one is not justified in de-
manding that a literary work must employ one or another
of these techniques before it can be called a midrash. To
fasten attention on the individual devices (e.g., gematria,
notrikon, etc.) and to set them up as criteria of midrash is
to become fascinated with a multiplicity of techniques and
to miss the basic operation underlying all of them. The
exegetical methods were employed by the rabbis in order
to show the sequence between the Scripture text and the
midrashic thought, and it is this indication of sequence which
is the only primary characteristic of midrash in the area
of method. How it is accomplished is secondary and
contingent upon the background and talents of the interpreter and upon the particular period in the history of the
development of midrash that the work comes from. [29]

---

29. That the specific rabbinic methods are secondary characteristics is borne out by the fact that in haggadic interpretation the
rabbis were not bound to specific rules. Rules of interpretation
were given (which were apparently no more than statements of
accepted practices of previous rabbis) but they were used only as
helpful guides, and the haggadist was free to use whatever means
suggested themselves in order to establish sequence. In other words
the important thing was the indication of sequence; the method
was secondary and up to the individual to find a cogent way to do it.
Moreover, many of the rabbinic rules of exegesis were derived from
pagan sources. As Saul Lieberman has demonstrated (*op. cit.* [see
n. 20] 68-82) a number of the rabbinic rules for biblical interpretation were current in the literary world at that time and even

It should be further noted here that the indication of sequence between text and midrashic statement is really less a requirement of midrash than it is a demand of the human mind. In other words, for the comment on the text to be meaningful to the audience it must appear to be related to the text in some way. Often in the midrashim the indication of sequence is not always explicit. The connection between comment and text is sometimes left unstated and the audience is expected to see the connection. And sometimes, as for example in the case of the frequent identification of Edom with Rome where the value assigned appears to be quite arbitrary, the interpretation is in fact based on a conventional value assigned to a term in the text. Consequently the explicit indication of sequence will not always appear in an interpretation and we must not make the indication of sequence a necessary element of the visible structure. The indication of sequence is necessary only logically and it may be accomplished implicitly.

We might also note that just because one finds rabbinic exegetical methods being employed in a given work, one is not necessarily in the presence of a midrash. For

---

relate back to hoary antiquity, for they were used by both Jews and non-Jews in the interpretation of dreams and by non-Jews in the interpretation of oracles as well. Hence many of the rules (and thus to a certain extent the whole method in which Scripture was approached) were not developed within the framework of midrash with an organic relationship to that literary form. Rather they were well-established devices that were resorted to by the rabbis in order to satisfy one of the demands of midrash, the indication of sequence between the text and the midrashic idea. And these particular methods were chosen simply because the argumentation produced by them would be familiar, understandable, and forceful to the interpreter's contemporaries.

example, the methods of creative historiography can be and were used in the service of free haggadah, and some of the methods of creative philology were used for the interpretation of dreams (see note 29 above).

With regard to exegetical method, some have proposed that *careful analysis* of the text is a primary characteristic of midrash. [30]   In the rabbinic midrash this certainly is a prominent feature.   However, every midrashic statement is not based on *careful* analysis, and it is conceivable that pre-rabbinic material might be found which does comment on a text but without attentive analysis of the words, etc. It would seem that such material should not thereby be excluded from the category midrash.   As with the note "creative," perhaps the best way to express the matter is that midrash *frequently* is characterized by a careful analysis of the biblical text, but any single midrashic statement may be an exception to the general rule.

6) Is *the note "Jewish"* a primary characteristic of midrash?   It would seem that Christian discussions of the OT in the NT and later Christian homiletic discussions of the Bible which manifest the other primary characteristics of midrash could legitimately be called midrash also.   Such literary works stand in the same tradition as the Jewish material as an offshoot of the parent stem, and the mere fact that the word midrash is Hebrew and that we have set up as the exemplar of our modern literary category the Jewish midrashim, should not deter us from seeing the two groups of literature as being two species of the same literary genre.

---

30. Bloch, *VDBS* 5, 1265-66; J. A. Fitzmyer, " 'Now This Melchizedek . . .' (Heb 7, 1)," *CBQ* 25 (1963) 305.

Samaritan works of the same type could also be called midrash. [31]

In her article in the *Dictionnaire de la Bible, Supplément,* Mlle. Bloch states that the fact that midrash takes its departure from Scripture excludes all possibility of finding parallels to this literary genre outside of Israel. Faith in a revelation which is consigned to sacred books is an essential prerequisite for writers of this literary form. [32] Recently, however, François Daumas has called attention to several previously published Egyptian works which seem to bear witness to the existence of a prophetic literature and the exegesis thereof in ancient Egypt. [33] One demotic papyrus dating perhaps from the beginning of the Ptolemaic period is a section-by-section commentary on an apparently prophetic document of the same period and bears strong resemblance to the Qumrân *pešārîm* in form and aim. Other material from Egypt bears witness to the explanatory glossing of prophetic texts as far back as the Middle Kingdom and the glossing of other material even earlier. The dependence of later Jewish midrash on such Egyptian material has yet to be established, but, if such a dependence does become clear, we can see no reason for refusing to classify the Egyptian material as midrash. Like the Christian material, the Egyptian would stand in the same tradition. If, however, the Egyptian material stands in a tradition independent of Jewish midrash, then the term midrash should be avoided

---

31. E.g., the Midrash of Marqah; cf. M. Heidenheim, *Der Commentar Marqah's des Samaritaners* (Weimar, 1896).

32. Bloch, *VDBS* 5, 1265.

33. F. Daumas, "Littérature prophétique et exégétique égyptienne et commentaires esséniens," *A la rencontre de Dieu: Mémorial Albert Gelin* (Le Puy, 1961) 203-21.

—or if it is used, it should be seen as an improper and analogous use in lieu of a better title.

We may summarize the discussion to this point by saying that rabbinic midrash is a literature concerned with the Bible; it is a literature about a literature. A midrash is a work that attempts to make a text of Scripture understandable, useful, and relevant for a later generation. It is the text of Scripture which is the point of departure, and it is for the sake of the text that the midrash exists. The treatment of any given text may be creative or non-creative, but the literature as a whole is predominantly creative in its handling of the biblical material. The interpretation is accomplished sometimes by rewriting the biblical material, sometimes by commenting upon it. In either case the midrash may go as far afield as it wishes provided that at some stage at least there is to be found some connection, implicit or explicit, between the biblical text and the new midrashic composition. At times this connection with the text may be convincing, at times it may be desperate; it is sufficient merely that a connection be there. Frequently the midrashic literature is characterized by a careful analysis of and attention to the biblical text.

Thus far we have been led by our investigation to concur with the statement of Renée Bloch that rabbinic midrash is homiletic reflection on the Bible which seeks to apply a given text of the past to present circumstances. [34] We would prefer to say "work" or "composition" or "literature" rather than "reflection" to make clear that we are speaking of the literary genre midrash and not of the exegetical method midrash or of the activity of biblical interpretation in general (an ambiguity frequent in Bloch's work); but aside from that

---

34. Bloch, *VDBS* 5, 1265-66.

we would agree with this one definition of Mlle. Bloch and with her statement that two primary characteristics of rabbinic midrash are "le rattachement et la référence constante à l'Écriture" and "l'adaptation au présent." [35]   The task which remains is to go back into the pre-rabbinic literature and find truly similar works in the same tradition with the same basic characteristics.   In this way we will build up our literary classification, and at the same time, by accepting or rejecting works for it, come to an even clearer notion of the genre.

---

35. *Ibid.*, 1266.

Chapter 4
Examples of Pre-Rabbinic Midrash

*I*n this final chapter we will indicate what in our judgment are true examples of the literary genre midrash prior to the rabbinic collections. The discussion here is in no way intended to be a complete inventory of all the examples in the literature of that period. Rather, we will point out significant examples of a variety of types of midrash to serve as a guide for future work and as an occasion for enunciating various principles and elements implicit in our conclusions above. At the same time and for the same purposes we will also discuss some works and passages which in our judgment are not midrashic but which have been classified as midrash in recent criticism. The procedure will be that of analysis and comparison, the two-fold method of genre study—analysis of the intentions of the author as manifested in the structure, content and tone of the literary piece under consideration, and comparison with other works to situate the piece in its proper tradition.

THE MIDRASH OF THE PASSOVER HAGGADAH

The most natural piece to single out first is the midrash on Dt 26, 5-8 in the Passover Haggadah, the liturgy for

Passover eve. Louis Finkelstein argues that the work dates from the last half of the third century B.C. or the first half of the second and inclines toward the former date. [1] Daube [2] and Seeligmann [3] opt for the latter. We give here the beginning of the midrash in Finkelstein's translation: [4]

Go forth and learn. What did Laban the Aramaean intend to do to our father, Jacob? For Pharaoh decreed the destruction only of the males, while Laban sought to destroy the whole family. Thus it is written, *The Aramaean sought to destroy my father and he (my father) went down into Egypt and sojourned there, few in number, and he became there a nation, great, mighty, and populous. And he went down into Egypt;* compelled thereto by the word of God.

And sojourned there. This teaches us that he did not go down into Egypt to settle there, but only to sojourn, as it is said, "And they said unto Pharaoh: To sojourn in the land are we come; for there is no pasture for thy servants' flocks; for the famine is sore in the land of Canaan. Now therefore let thy servants dwell in the land of Goshen" (Gn 47, 4).

---

1. L. Finkelstein, "The Oldest Midrash: Pre-Rabbinic Ideals and Teachings in the Passover Haggadah," *HarvTR* 31 (1938) 291-317.

2. D. Daube, "The Earliest Structure of the Gospels," *NTS* 5 (1959) 176, 179, n. 4.

3. I. L. Seeligmann, *The Septuagint Version of Isaiah* (Leiden, 1948) 85-86.—S. Stein, "The Influence of Symposia Literature on the Literary Form of the Pesaḥ Haggadah," *JJS* 8 (1957) 13-44, dates it in the second or third Christian century, but his argument is from silence and is extremely weak.

4. Finkelstein, *art. cit.*, 295-98.

Few in number, as it is said, "Thy fathers went down into Egypt with threescore and ten persons; and now the Lord thy God hath made thee as the stars of heaven for multitude" (Dt 10, 22).

And he became there a nation. This teaches us that the Israelites were distinguished there.

Great and mighty, as it is said, "And the children of Israel were fruitful and multiplied, and waxed exceedingly mighty, and the land was filled with them" (Ex 1, 7).

And populous, as it is said, "I caused thee to increase, even as the growth of the field; and thou didst increase and grow up, and thou camest to excellent beauty" (Ez 16, 7).

And the Egyptians dealt ill with us, as it is said, "Come let us deal wisely with them lest they multiply, and it come to pass that, when there befalleth us any war, they also join themselves unto our enemies, and fight against us, and get them up out of the land" (Ex 1, 10).

And afflicted us, as it is said, "Therefore they did set over them taskmasters to afflict them with their burdens. And they built for Pharaoh store-cities, Pithom and Raamses" (*ibid.* 1, 11) . . . .

The work comments on each detail of the text, enriching it and applying it to the contemporary situation,[5] often with the help of other Scripture passages. It is similar in form to the later exegetical midrashim, although much simpler in that multiple citations from the Scriptures and assembling of interpretations of the rabbis are lacking.

---

5. See Finkelstein, *art. cit.,* where he discusses at length the historical background of the midrash and the possible significance of the interpretative remarks.

THE *Pešārîm*

Soon after the discovery and publication of the biblical commentaries from Qumrân the question arose as to whether or not these commentaries (or *pešārîm* as they have come to be called) should or could be called midrash.   Three positions have been taken over the years: that they are not midrash, that they are midrash, and that they are midrash pesher (in contradistinction to midrash haggadah and midrash halakah).   The discussion is still joined from time to time, authors siding with one or other of these positions.

Those who deny the propriety of the use of the term midrash in connection with the *pešārîm* have done so for various reasons.   Millar Burrows states that "midrash is a homiletic expansion of a biblical book or part of a book for the purpose of edification" and that its method of exposition is either like a popular expository lecture in which the opinions of various authors are cited and problems of exegesis discussed or like the telling of a Bible story.   The Habakkuk *pēšer* does not have this structure and form and therefore is better labeled a commentary. [6]   J. L. Teicher refused to call the Habakkuk *pēšer* a midrash because its aim is different from that of the midrashim in that the purpose of the *pēšer* is to show how certain significant events represent the unravelling of the mysteries of the prophetic utterances.   Thus the *pēšer* should be called an apocalyptic commentary. [7]   Geza Vermes writing in 1951

---

6. M. Burrows, *The Dead Sea Scrolls* (New York, 1955) 211. Cf. also Burrows' further remarks in W. H. Brownlee, "Biblical Interpretation Among the Sectaries of the Dead Sea Scrolls," *BA* 14 (1951) 76.

7. J. L. Teicher, "The Dead Sea Scrolls—Documents of the Jewish-Christian Sect of Ebionites," *JJS* 2 (1951) 76.

agreed with Teicher because he felt that midrash is an
exegetical research either to establish law from the Bible
(halakah) or to discover in the Bible moral or religious
teachings (haggadah). [8]   In 1954, Vermes again held that
the pēšer is not a midrash, but this time because the
pēšer differs in structure from the midrashim in that the
pēšer is a paraphrase of a biblical text and not a "more or
less independent development as is often the case in midrāš."
Moreover, the pēšer does not cite other biblical books or
the opinions of teachers. [9]   Karl Elliger in his work on the
Habakkuk pēšer insisted that the pēšer differs from midrash
in that the interpretations of the pēšer are not derived essen-
tially from the text but merely stand "neben dem Text."
Moreover, the structure of the pēšer is less detailed and
developed than that of the midrash. [10]   Cecil Roth felt that
the attempt to characterize the pēšer literature as midrash
leaves out of account the principal characteristic of the
pēšer: that it does not elucidate the biblical text as does
midrash but determines the application of certain biblical
prophecies to current and even contemporary events. [11]
Dupont-Sommer defines midrash as "stories depending on
'haggadic' traditions" and "purely imaginary developments"
on Scripture and sees this as differing radically from the

---

8. G. Vermes, "Le 'Commentaire d'Habacuc' et le Nouveau
Testament," Cahiers Sioniens 5 (1951) 344-45.

9. Id., "A propos des Commentaires bibliques découverts à Qumrân," La Bible et l'Orient: Travaux du premier congrès d'archéologie
et d'orientalisme bibliques (Saint-Cloud 23-25 avril 1954) (Paris,
1955) 96-97.

10. K. Elliger, Studien zum Habakuk-Kommentar vom Toten
Meer (Tübingen, 1953) 163-64.

11. C. Roth, "The Subject Matter of Qumrân Exegesis," VT 10
(1960) 51-52.

genre of the *pešārîm*. The *pešārîm* "aim at discovering predictions in the biblical text relating to the end of the world, whereas the *midrashim* endeavor to make the story of the past more vivid and full."[12] Carmignac refuses them the name midrash (which he defines as edifying glosses to make the word of God relevant) because the *pešārîm* seek to reveal the hidden meaning of prophetic texts to which are attributed symbolic values.[13]

Another group of authors has insisted that the *pešārîm* are very definitely midrash, and again for a variety of reasons: Brownlee because the exegesis of the *pešārîm* is midrashic;[14] Seeligmann[15] and Delcor[16] because the *pēšer* actualizes Sacred Scripture; Bloch because it actualizes Scripture and uses midrashic techniques;[17] Silberman because the aim of the *pēšer* and its method and structure can be found in the midrashim;[18] Michel because it is history written in the light of earlier history as found and interpreted in a book of the Bible.[19]   Milik,[20] Allegro,[21] and van der

---

12. A. Dupont-Sommer, *The Essene Writings from Qumran*, trans. by G. Vermes (Cleveland, 1962) 280-81, 310.

13. J. Carmignac, É. Cothenet et H. Lignée, *Les textes de Qumran*, II (Paris, 1963) 46.

14. Brownlee, *art. cit.*, 76.

15. I. L. Seeligmann, "Voraussetzungen der Midraschexegese," *SupplVT* I (Leiden, 1953) 171, n. 1.

16. M. Delcor, *Essai sur le midrash d'Habacuc* (Paris, 1951) 77.

17. R. Bloch, "Midrash," *VDBS* 5, 1277.

18. L. H. Silberman, "Unriddling the Riddle," *RevQum* (1961) 323-64.

19. A. Michel, *Le Maître de Justice* (Avignon, 1954) 26-28.

20. J. T. Milik, "Fragments d'un midrash de Michée dans les manuscrits de Qumrân," *RB* 59 (1952) 413, n. 4.

21. J. M. Allegro, "Fragments of a Qumran Scroll of Eschatological *Midrāšîm*," *JBL* 78 (1958) 350.

Ploeg [22] call the $p^e\check{s}\bar{a}r\hat{i}m$ midrash but in Qumrân's generic sense of the term ("exegesis, interpretation") and not in the rabbinic or modern technical sense. Daumas follows van der Ploeg but also sees in the $p^e\check{s}\bar{a}r\hat{i}m$ a genuine midrashic search for hidden meanings in the Scriptures. [23] Lane reserves the term midrash for the complex type $p\bar{e}\check{s}er$ only (4QF1), since Qumrân used it and since this is a convenient way to distinguish this type of $p\bar{e}\check{s}er$ from the simple ones—but midrash "in the Qumran rather than the rabbinic sense of the term, i.e., with the same messianic, eschatological orientation as much of the rest of their literature." [24]

In 1953, Brownlee suggested a new classificaion, midrash pesher, by which the $p^e\check{s}\bar{a}r\hat{i}m$ might be both related to (on the basis of type of exegesis) and distinguished from (on the basis of style and content) the previously known rabbinic midrashim of the classes midrash halakah and midrash haggadah. [25] This classification has been adopted by Krister Stendahl who uses it apparently to relate the $p^e\check{s}\bar{a}r\hat{i}m$ to rabbinic midrash on the basis of the "realistic nature" of $p\bar{e}\check{s}er$ interpretation and to distinguish them from rabbinic

22. J. van der Ploeg, "Le rouleau d'Habacuc de la grotte de 'Ain Fešha," *BO* 8 (1951) 2; *id.*, "Les manuscrits de Désert de Juda. Livres récents," *BO* 16 (1959) 163.

23. F. Daumas, "Littérature prophétique et exégétique égyptienne et commentaires esséniens," *A la rencontre de Dieu: Mémorial Albert Gelin* (Le Puy, 1961) 204-5.

24. W. R. Lane, "A New Commentary Structure in 4Q Florilegium," *JBL* 78 (1959), 346.

25. W. H. Brownlee, *The Dead Sea Habakkuk Midrash and the Targum of Jonathan* (mimeographed; Duke University, Feb. 2, 1953). Cf. also the same article, somewhat revised: "The Habakkuk Midrash and the Targum of Jonathan," *JJS* 7 (1956) 179, n. 38.

midrash because of their sectarian character. [26] The same classification is used by Grelot who sees the midrash pesher as differing from haggadah and halakah in that it actualizes prophetic Scriptures (and eventually other types) in showing their accomplishment in the events of the near past and present in order to infer what will happen in the future. [27]

From all of these discussions it becomes clear that the problem lies in two areas: the definition of midrash and the mode of expressing the very real differences between *pēšer* and midrash. An assortment of definitions of midrash has been brought to the discussion, and sometimes the definitions of midrash have been rather limited and restricted; one wonders if it is not sometimes a case in which authors, seeing the real difference between the *pēšer* and the midrash and trying to express this difference, consciously or unconsciously construct definitions of midrash which result in the exclusion of the *pēšer* from the genre midrash.

We would unhesitatingly classify the *pᵉšārîm* as belonging to the literary genre midrash—simply because the *pᵉšārîm* actualize biblical texts, make them meaningful for the sect, and show where the secrets of the sect are to be found in the Scriptures. The biblical text is the point of departure throughout the material and that for the sake of which the *pēšer* exists, and that is sufficient to make it midrash. Moreover, the striking similarity in structure, method and aim between the *pēšer* and the *petirah* found in the later midrashim [28]

---

26. K. Stendahl, *The School of St. Matthew* (Uppsala, 1954) 184.

27. P. Grelot, "L'interprétation catholique des livres saints," *Introduction à la Bible*, éds. A. Robert et A. Feuillet, I (Tournai, 1957) 175.

28. Silberman, *art. cit.*

confirms the judgment that the *pēšer* stands in the midrashic tradition.

How should the secondary differences between the *pēšer* and rabbinic midrash be expressed? Certainly the threefold division: midrash haggadah, midrash halakah and midrash pesher is not satisfactory and should be abandoned. [29] The classifications halakah and haggadah are based upon content (legal vs. non-legal discussion of a text) and are mutually exclusive terms as set up by the rabbis. There is not room for another classification according to content—least of all for one that signifies messianic, eschatological content, for that sort of thing can be found in the rabbinic midrashim as has been pointed out above. [30] The *pᵉšārîm,* then, are haggadic midrash. Perhaps the terms "Qumrân" or "Essene" midrash could express the secondary differences. Or since the term *pēšer* (which is our modern designation and not Qumrân's) will probably continue to be used to designate the Qumrân commentaries, perhaps it can serve as a convenient designation for the secondary characteristics peculiar to these works (whether these be in the area of method, or the sectarian aspect, or even content provided that in the latter case the term *pēšer* is not seen as opposed to haggadah and halakah). Even the term "midrash pesher" would not be unacceptable if it is freed from the tripartite content division it has been associated with and used in some other connection.

THE PALESTINIAN TARGUMS

Unlike the Targum Onkelos and the Targum on Job from Qumrân, the Pentateuchal targums from Palestine in

---

29. Thus similarly Silberman, *art. cit.,* 328, n. 10.
30. P. 68 and n. 27.

so far as we can recover them (and to some extent the Targum Jonathan on the prophets) contain, in addition to the
Aramaic rendering of the biblical text, narrative and other
expansions on the text, probably reflecting the synagogal
homilies which followed the reading of the Bible. Renée
Bloch has suggested that the Palestinian targums on the
Pentateuch especially are for this reason much closer to
a midrash than to a version, [31] and that they are in fact
the point of departure of midrash properly speaking since
they contain, in a less developed stage, its structure and its
essential themes. [32] Certainly the sections of expansions
in these targums are midrash, but that the whole targum
should be called a midrash is open to question. It is true
that the material brought to the text comes from the same
synagogal tradition as does much of the material in the later
midrashic collections and that the targums as a whole
actualize Scripture, but to call these targums midrash and
thus distinguish them from the more literal ones is to use as
a criterion of genre solely the ratio between text and expansion. The distinction between targum and midrash, however, is much more basic. The purpose of the targum is to
give translation plus incidental material; the purpose of the
midrash is to give homiletic material with incidental connection to the text. And this purpose is often reflected in the
outward form: a targum sets out to give the full biblical text
whereas a midrash frequently does not. There is good
reason, then, to retain the traditional title targum for the more

31. R. Bloch, *VDBS* 5, 1278-79.

32. R. Bloch, "Note sur l'utilisation des fragments de la Geniza
du Caire pour l'étude du Targum Palestinien," *Revue des études
juives*, Nouvelle Série 14 [114] (1955) 6-7. For a more detailed
description of the characteristics of these targums see R. Le Déaut,
La nuit pascale (Rome, 1963) 58-62.

fulsome ones and to speak of them as targums with midrashic sections.

THE BIBLICAL ANTIQUITIES OF PSEUDO-PHILO

Pseudo-Philo's *Liber Antiquitatum Biblicarum* (LAB), which is at least as old as the first Christian century,[33] is a retelling of biblical history from Adam to the death of Saul. The narrative follows closely that of the OT but passes rapidly over many incidents and omits many sections, while on the other hand it elaborates certain portions (especially the period of the Judges) and furnishes many novel additions to the narrative of the Bible including genealogies, lengthy speeches and songs. Because in all the MSS the work ends rather abruptly with (in the midst of?) the speech of the dying Saul, it has been suggested that Pseudo-Philo's story originally went beyond Saul and that the ending has

---

33. The work is known to us only in a Latin translation based upon a lost Greek translation made at the end of the first Christian century from a likewise lost Hebrew original which was perhaps older. The *editio princeps* is that of J. Sichardus (Bâle, 1527). The work has been translated into English by M. R. James (*The Biblical Antiquities of Philo* [London, 1917]) and into German by P. Riessler (*Altjüdisches Schrifttum ausserhalb der Bibel* [Augsburg, 1928] 735-861). The Latin text has been republished by G. Kisch (*Pseudo-Philo's Liber Antiquitatum Biblicarum* [Notre Dame, 1949]). Useful studies of the work are L. Cohn, "An Apocryphal Work Ascribed to Philo of Alexandria," *JQR* 10 (1898/99) 277-332; A. Spiro, "Samaritans, Tobiads, and Judahites in Pseudo-Philo," *Proceedings of the American Academy for Jewish Research* 20 (1951) 279-355; O. Eissfeldt, "Zur Kompositionstechnik des Pseudo-Philonischen Liber Antiquitatum Biblicarum," *Interpretationes ad vetus testamentum pertinentes Sigmundo Mowinckel septuagenario missae* (Oslo, 1955) 52-71.

been lost. [34]   On the other hand, Riessler and Spiro insist
that the work as we have it is integral and, because LAB ends
where the narrative of Chr begins, they suggest that it was
intended as a supplement to Chr for the earlier history and
that it is of the same historical genre. [35]   Spiro speculates
that it was intended as a popular work for circles which were
not familiar with Jos-Sm but only with the highlights of the
Pentateuch and with Chr.   The material in Gn-Sm told
of many strange things in the days of old (the escapades of
various figures, opposition to the monarchy, lack of Mosaic
institutions, etc.) and there was a need for someone to handle
this history in the same selective way that the Chronicler
had handled the later period.   LAB was the result.   Spiro
also suggests that LAB is a polemical work against Samaritans
and Tobiads.

The polemical dimension of LAB seems quite secondary.
However, there is no doubt that Pseudo-Philo is concerned
about many of the strange things in early Israel and that he
is using the same techniques as the Chronicler (selection of
narratives, insertion of extra-biblical material) and like the
Chronicler he is using history as a basis for exhortation.   But
the more basic questions are: did Pseudo-Philo see himself
as writing a book like Chr or did he see himself as a midrashist gathering material of interest on the margin of the
biblical text?   These are extremely difficult questions to
answer.   Our task would be made somewhat easier if we
were sure of the condition of the ending of LAB.   But even
if LAB as we now have it is intact and even if Chr suggested

---

34. Sixtus Senensis, *Bibliotheca Sancta* (Cologne, 1576) 314.
James (*op. cit.*, 19-20, 61-65, 185, 187) and Kisch (*op. cit.*, 29)
accept this as a fact.

35. Spiro, *art. cit.*; similarly Riessler, *op. cit.*, 1315.

the terminus of the work, this need not indicate that LAB is of the same genre, for Pseudo-Philo could have conceived of it as a supplement to Chr but a supplement by way of a midrashic collection. And this in fact seems to be the case. If Pseudo-Philo was trying to do for Gn-Sm what Chr did for the later material, he has done a very skimpy job in many areas, and all the omissions of material from the biblical story are not accounted for on polemical grounds as Spiro attempts to do. Moreover, a large amount of the content consists of amplifications on the biblical narrative. On this account LAB seems to be some distance from the type of work Chr is (regardless of how Chr affected LAB in extent or method), and with the work as we have it as our only clue it seems better to see it primarily as a summary retelling of the biblical account for the purpose of inserting where desirable extra-biblical material for edification and for expansion's sake. With regard to extent of coverage there is a certain similarity between LAB and the much later *Sefer ha-Yashar* which runs from Adam to the Judges. On the basis of the present evidence, then, we would call LAB a narrative midrash.

THE GENESIS APOCRYPHON

The *Genesis Apocryphon* (GA) has been classified by some as a targum because it presents a rendering of the Hebrew text of Gn into Aramaic. [36] Because of its ex-

---

36. M. Black, "The Recovery of the Language of Jesus," *NTS* 3 (1956-57) 310-13; M. R. Lehmann, "1Q Genesis Apocryphon in the Light of the Targumim and Midrashim," *RevQum* 1 (1958) 251 (a midrashic targum).

pansions on the biblical text [37] the work has been called by others a midrash, a primitive and simple forerunner of the later more elaborate rabbinic narrative midrashim. [38] Milik refuses to classify it as either targum or midrash and sees it as a compilation of traditional lore on the patriarchs preserving the popular literary form of the pseudepigraph (the patriarchs themselves being the narrators). [39] The editors

---

37. The nature of the text and its relation to Gn can be seen in G. Vermes' *Scripture and Tradition in Judaism* (Leiden, 1961) 97-110 where he arranges GA, cols. 19-22, and Gn in parallel columns.

In some cases the embellishments on Gn serve to make the biblical account more real and vivid. Thus, in 19, 11-13 geographical data are given to fill in the biblical lacuna; in 20, 2-8 the summary statement of Gn (12, 15) is expanded to explain how the Egyptian princes praised Sarah's beauty, as well as to give the number of princes and the name of one of them. Other embellishments serve to make the account more edifying, such as the addition in 20, 12-16 on Abraham's confidence in God and in 22, 25 on the benevolence of Abraham. Other expansions seek to harmonize the Gn account with other biblical texts: hence the mention of Hagar in GA 20, 32 (to harmonize with the note in Gn 16, 1 that she was an Egyptian maid); hence, also, the addition in GA 21, 15f. (to make Abraham take the journey that he was just commanded to take and which the Bible seems to imply that he didn't), and the addition of the escape of the King of Sodom in 21, 32 (to explain his reappearance in Gn 14, 17). In some cases geographical locations are identified (GA 21, 23-25. 29). Some additions provide reasons for actions. Thus, in 19, 10 it is explained why Abraham went to Egypt and not elsewhere: he had heard there was corn in Egypt; in 19, 14-17 the dream of Abraham is supplied to explain what prompted Abraham to fear for his life and thus conceal Sarah's identity; and in 20, 22-23 it is explained how Pharaoh discovered Sarah's identity: Lot told him. Finally, the author of GA is at pains to allay any doubts that the biblical text might raise (e.g., in GA 20, 17 it is emphasized that Sarah was protected) and also he seeks to remove anything unfitting in the text (e.g., in GA 20, 10 Abraham owes his life to Sarah but not his wealth as Gn states; in GA the gifts come to Abraham in return for his curing the Pharaoh [20, 31-33]).

For a discussion of these and other features of the text see N. Avigad and Y. Yadin, *A Genesis Apocryphon. A Scroll from the Wilderness of Judaea* (Jerusalem, 1956) 23-37; Vermes, *op. cit.,* 110-121; Lehmann, *art. cit.;* G. Sarfatti, "Notes on the Genesis Apocryphon," *Tarbiz* 28 (1959) 254-59; Carmignac, *et al., op. cit.,* II, 221-40.

Since this was written there has appeared the detailed study of Joseph A. Fitzmyer, *The* Genesis Apocryphon *of Qumran Cave I. A Commentary* (Rome, 1966), which is now the most useful tool available for the study of GA as well as of its relation to the text of Gn. With regard to genre Fitzmyer concludes that GA has a strong relationship to targum and midrash and stands somewhere between them with a definite relation to works like Enoch, Jubilees, the Testament of the Twelve Patriarchs, etc. It is thus an example of a type of late Jewish narrative writing strongly inspired by the canonical Scriptures but abundantly enhanced with imaginative details (pp. 8-10). This is similar to our own view but we would place GA closer to a midrash and not stress the relationship to En, Jub and TestXII. The latter works, while containing midrashic elements (see below n. 102 on Jub), are very complex from the viewpoint of literary form and seem to stand at considerable distance from the much simpler GA. En, Jub and TestXII have strong apocalyptic elements (for which there is meagre evidence in GA; see Fitzmyer, p. 12) and TestXII seemingly belongs to a genre of its own (testament) while containing other genres within its framework.

38. P. Kahle, *The Cairo Geniza* (Oxford, [2]1959) 198, having previously termed it a targum; Vermes, *op. cit.;* H. Lignée in Carmignac, *et al., op. cit.,* II, 215; Dupont-Sommer, *op. cit.,* 280; G. Lambert, "Une 'Genèse Apocryphe' trouvée à Qumrân," *La secte de Qumrân et les origines du christianisme* (*Recherches Bibliques* IV; Bruges, 1959) 105.

39. J. T. Milik, *Ten Years of Discovery in the Wilderness of Judaea* (Studies in Biblical Theology 26; London, 1959) 31.

of the preliminary edition have termed it an apocryphon since it is a sort of apocryphal version of stories from Gn. [40]

For a discussion of literary genre we are at a distinct disadvantage in not possessing the beginning and end of GA. From what we do know of the work it very much resembles a targum in that it sets out to give the full biblical text, [41] rather literally for Gn 14, and elsewhere in much the same free and paraphrastic way that characterizes many sections of the Pentateuchal Palestinian targums. But the autobiographical form found in some sections of GA is not a normal targumic feature, and this may be an indication that the nature of the work is other than targumic. The autobiographical feature is one held in common with testaments and other literature [42] and may indicate that GA is a collection (the autobiographical feature is not constant) of assorted material to elucidate the biblical text and expand on it in the spirit of LAB, for certainly a large number of alterations and additions to the biblical text are for exegetical purposes. GA seems to stand somewhere between a targum and LAB and its resemblance to a targum may be due to its primitive and simple form. Perhaps the nature of the work will become clearer when the complete MS is published as well as other similar texts from Qumrân. At present, it can be said that the expansions on Gn in GA are certainly midrash and that there is some degree of probability to the view that the whole work is.

---

40. Avigad and Yadin, *op. cit.*, 8, 38.
41. Save for Gn 13, 6. 8-10. 13.
42. See Lignée, *op. cit.*, 212-15.

SOME NON-MIDRASHIC NARRATIVES

Other writers also retold the biblical accounts by excerpting from the Scriptures and enlarging upon the biblical data, but the literary form of many of these works is not midrash.

1. A clear example is Josephus' *Jewish Antiquities* (JA), especially in the part of JA that deals with the period from creation to the exile (Bks. 1-10), where Josephus uses as his source the biblical books as well as a considerable amount of traditional lore on Jewish history. JA is not a midrash on the historical books of the OT; it does not stand in relation to the biblical books utilized as for example GA does to Gn. Rather, Josephus has written a history of the Jewish people and this is evident from two features of the work. First of all, JA is clearly modeled after the *Roman Antiquities* of Dionysius of Halicarnassus (as to title, number of books, and in some cases style [43]), and the author evidently sees himself as writing in that tradition. Secondly, in the preface the author does not indicate any intention of interpreting the Jewish Scriptures but states explicitly that he is writing a history (JA I, 1) and that the primary motive for writing the work was to inform the pagan world of the history of the Jews (I, 3-4), a secondary motive being to show that God blesses those who keep His law (I, 14). In order to accomplish these aims he will set forth the details as found in the Scripture record (I, 17). Hence, the biblical material utilized by Josephus is not looked upon as an object to be clarified, interpreted and made relevant; it is rather a source

---

43. H. St. J. Thackeray, *Josephus*, IV (London, 1930), ix-x.

from which to draw material. Josephus does not intend his work to contribute anything by way of understanding to the biblical account; it is the biblical account which contributes to the work of Josephus. Therefore, JA as a whole is not a midrash, nor are those sections which contain fictional embellishments taken from targums and similar works. This legendary material was very likely used to interpret the biblical narrative in Josephus' sources in the manner of GA and is very useful for tracing the history of midrashic traditions, but Josephus has taken it over and used it as data for his history; hence, the material, now no longer in the service of the biblical text, ceases to be midrashic.

JA exemplifies very clearly the role that context plays in some literary genres—to the extent that in some cases the genre of a composition, or of an element of it if it is a composite work, is determined entirely by its context. [44] For example, the little story that Nathan tells David in 2 Sm 12, 1-4 about the poor man and his ewe lamb is in itself true enough to life to be a narration of fact and indeed is so understood by David at first ("The man who has done this deserves to die"). In the context of ordinary factual speech, then, it would be a factual narrative. When it is put in the context of "You are the man," the same composition becomes an allegory. The same story could be put in another context and could conceivably become a parable with a moral lesson for anyone. The story would be textually the same in each case; only the context would change and with it the literary form. In 2 Sm 14 the literary form of the plea of the woman of Tekoa is "drama" and this because

---

44. Cf. L. Alonso-Schökel, "Genera litteraria," *VD* 38 (1960) 1-15.

the context so determines it (vv. 2-3 for the reader; vv.
13ff. for the king). In another context the same words
could be a narration of fact. Context, then, plays a role
in the determining of the literary form of a composition,
and this is especially true of midrash. Conceivably, both
of the above compositions could be prefixed by some ap-
propriate biblical text and, thus put into the context of a
commentary on Scripture, would become a midrash. And
conversely the embellishments in Josephus which were once
probably in the context of the interpretation of Scripture now
are in the context of a history and cease to be midrashic.

2. Another example of the non-midrashic rewriting of
the biblical text are the Books of Chronicles—*pace* Robert,
Bloch and others. [45] The usual reason for classifying Chr
as a midrash is that Chr is an elaboration on and a free
handling of ancient texts and traditions in order to edify,
teach, and explain. It is pointed out that the Chronicler
is an historian and that the work is to some degree a history;
but it is also pointed out that the Chronicler "selects, emphasizes, and imaginatively embroiders the facts at his
disposal and to this degree he is a midrashic author." [46]

It is true that about half of Chr is dependent upon prior

---

45. A. Robert, "The Literary Genres," *Guide to the Bible,* vol.
1 (Paris, [2]1960) 508; R. Bloch, *VDBS* 5, 1271; P. Ellis, *The Men and
the Message of the Old Testament* (Collegeville, 1963) 260; H.
Lusseau, "Les livres des Chroniques," *Introduction à la Bible,* I
(Tournai, 1957) 722-23; L. Hartman, *Encyclopedic Dictionary of
the Bible* (New York, 1963) 365; J. Myers, *I Chronicles* (New York,
1965) xviii; etc.

46. Ellis, *op. cit.,* p. 260; the same ideas are expressed by the
others.

Scripture [47] and that the Chronicler has reworked and added to that Scripture and with a certain freedom in some areas— although not in the wholesale fictional manner that some like Pfeiffer would suggest, [48] for today we realize that some of the Chronicler's additions contain reliable historical material.   But was the purpose of the Chronicler to fill out the data of Sm-Kgs as GA did for Gn?   Is he truly a midrashic author?

The question of the primary objective of the Chronicler is not an easy one to answer.   Freedman has analyzed the structure and themes of Chr and concludes that the principal objective of the Chronicler was to write a history of the dynasty of David, especially its accomplishments in the religious and specifically the cultic areas, and to establish legitimate patterns of institutions and their personnel for the people of God.   It is around these fundamental points that the Chronicler constructs his history and theology. [49]

---

47. A list of the passages the Chronicler selected from Sm-Kgs is given in Myers, *op. cit.*, xlix-lxiii; *id., II Chronicles* (New York, 1965) xxiv-xxxii; E. L. Curtis and A. A. Madsen, *The Books of Chronicles* (ICC; New York, 1910) 17-19.   The method of the Chronicler and his use of his sources can be studied most easily in P. Vannutelli, *Libri Synoptici Veteris Testamenti* (Romae, 1931), and a useful guide for the study is A. Brunet, "Le Chroniste et ses sources," *RB* 60 (1953) 481-508; 61 (1954) 349-86.   The Chronicler has of course used the Old Palestinian text of the Deuteronomic history current in Jerusalem in his day, and it is by no means identical with the received text; see F. M. Cross, "The History of the Biblical Text in the Light of Discoveries in the Judaean Desert," *HarvTR* 57 (1964) 292-97.

48. R. H. Pfeiffer, *Introduction to the Old Testament* (London, 1952) 806; *id., IDB* 1, 578-80.

49. D. N. Freedman, "The Chronicler's Purpose," *CBQ* 23 (1961) 436-42.

Freedman's conclusions are rather convincingly argued. But even if one does not agree with him in every detail, it seems hard to construe the Chronicler's work as anything other than a history and a theology of history quite independent of the Deuteronomic history. In borrowing material from Sm-Kgs and combining it with material from elsewhere, the Chronicler has not sought to make a fuller, clearer, more interesting, trouble free version of Sm-Kgs and, thus, to write something for those books similar to GA. He has written a new work, a history of the Davidic dynasty, which has preoccupations which are not those of Sm-Kgs as well as new doctrinal themes which he is attempting to illustrate. The work is structured not on Sm-Kgs but according to the themes of the Chronicler. And all indications point to the fact that in taking material from Sm-Kgs the Chronicler is using those books as sources and not as an object of interpretation. He takes selected passages in accord with his interests, sometimes rearranges their order, abbreviates them, supplements them from extra-biblical sources or his own imagination, and practically all of his additions to the biblical text are for the purpose of throwing into relief one theme or another that is dear to the Chronicler.

It is true that some of the methods used by the Chronicler are the same as those to be used later by the author of GA and the rabbis in their narrative midrashim. But this is not a reason to call Chr midrash, for these methods are used by the authors of many literary forms. Selection of material and emphasis of details are methods employed by all historians, ancient and modern; and fiction in its various uses is a device that is common to several genres (e.g., popular pre-history, popular history, parable, apocalyptic, folklore, didactic fiction, and midrash if the fiction is at the service of a biblical text). As Seeligmann has pointed out, many of the techniques used in rabbinic midrash (alteration of traditions, play on words, adaptation of biblical texts) are found in use in the OT. [50]   But they are all techniques and can be used for many purposes, and the literary form midrash does not have a monopoly on them.   Technique and method, therefore, are not to be confused with literary form.

Nor should we classify Chr as a midrash because the Chronicler used the Midrash of the Book of the Kings and the Midrash of the Prophet Iddo as sources for his extra-biblical material.   As was already stated, we have no idea of the nature of these two "midrashim" mentioned in Chr, but even if they were something like GA and were to be classified under the modern literary category, midrash, this would still not mean that Chr is a midrash any more than JA is a midrash because Josephus borrowed material from midrashic works.   The material borrowed would have been at the service of the Bible in the original midrash, but in Chr it is used as data to fill out a new work of history.   The context of the material is now entirely different.

It must be admitted that midrash and history are not always easy to distinguish.   History is concerned with the interpretation of events; midrash is concerned with the interpretation of texts.   Whenever the object of discussion is clearly one or the other, there is, of course, no difficulty in ascertaining the genre of a work.   Frequently, however, the texts which are the subject of a midrash are narratives dealing with events and, thus, there is an interest in the events related (GA, and Wis 11-19 discussed below).   Likewise, the events which are the subject of a history are not infrequently known to the historian from earlier texts and are recounted by reproducing these earlier sources in part

---

50. I. L. Seeligmann, *art. cit.* (see n. 15 above) 150-81.

or in whole (Chr and JA). In borderline areas such as these it is sometimes very difficult in practice to classify a work according to genre. In theory, at least, the general rule can be given that a midrash will be distinguishable by its interest not in events *simpliciter* but in events as related in a specific way in a given text, and that a characteristic feature of a midrash will be either its skimpy presentation of the text to provide a framework within which to introduce ample embellishments at various points (LAB) or its attention to details of a narrative (GA) as opposed to a recasting and restructuring of older material in one way or another (JA, Chr) as is characteristic of a history.

3. It has been suggested that the historical psalms (Pss 78; 106; etc.) should be classified as midrash, [51] but these are actually recitals of salvation history. In Ps 78, 5-7 the psalmist states the *lex narrationis*: "He set it up as a decree in Jacob and established it as a law in Israel that what he commanded our fathers they should make known to their sons ... that they might not forget the deeds of God but keep his commands" (cf. Ex 13, 8; Dt 4, 9; 6, 20ff.; Jgs 6, 13); and it is in this light that the historical psalms and other similar short narrations of biblical history such as Sirach's Praise of the Fathers, [52] Wis 10, CD 2, 14-3,

---

51. Bloch, *VDBS* 5, 1275.

52. Siebeneck (*CBQ* 21 [1959] 416), following Bloch (*VDBS* 5, 1274), calls Sirach's Praise of the Fathers (44, 1-50, 24) an historical psalm but says it should also be called haggadic midrash because Sirach uses Scripture, exploits and reorganizes it to make it an instrument of edification in the light of contemporary needs. It is also pointed out that "midrash is what Sirach himself calls his teaching in 51, 23." It would be more accurate to say that, if the text as we have it is original, Sirach calls his book or his teaching a *bêt hammidrāš* or school, and, of course, this is irrelevant

19, Acts 7 and Heb 11 should be read. These works are much closer in genre to the credos of Dt 6, 21-23; 26, 5-9 and to the historical prologue of a covenant renewal (Jos 24) or of a prayer (Neh 9, 6-31) than they are to GA and LAB, for it seems clear that it is the events and personages themselves and not some specific biblical narration of them which are the object of interest. The works are not a literature about a literature.

4. Besides those works which retell the biblical narrative there is another group of literature which is frequently termed midrash, namely, works of didactic fiction such as Est, Tb and Jon. [53] Apparently the sole reason for classifying these writings in this manner is that these works freely elaborate for didactic purposes an historical nucleus of one sort or another or are simply fiction. It is hard to see how this type of writing can be called midrash. Est, for example, stands in relation to no biblical text as, say, GA does to Gn, yet this is the essential note of midrash. If

---

to a discussion of the literary genre of any part of Sir, even prescinding from the fact that Sirach's use of the word *midrāš* is quite different from our modern technical literary term. In fact, the Praise of the Fathers is a recital of events similar to the historical psalms. Sirach begins his praise of Israel's ancestors with a statement of purpose (44, 1-15) in conformity with the literary procedure of his time. He intends to "praise those godly men, our ancestors" (v. 1) in the same way others had done: "at gatherings their wisdom is retold and the assembly sings their praises" (v. 15). This is the tradition in which he is writing. The poem addresses Solomon (47, 14ff.) and Elijah (48, 4ff.) in the second person and for this reason some have chosen to speak of the Praise of the Fathers as a eulogy.

53. Thus Robert, *Guide to the Bible,* 508; Lusseau, "Les autres hagiographes," *Introduction à la Bible,* I, 692; Ellis, *op. cit.,* 454-61; and others.

we are to be precise in our classification of literary works, we must avoid using midrash as a euphemism for biblical fiction and we should borrow from the rabbis the term (free) haggadah as well as the term midrash and use the term haggadah to describe works such as Est.

We would suggest the same classification of haggadah for Tb, even though there is some relation with Gn since some details in Tb have been borrowed from the stories of the patriarchs. But it is a standard technique of fiction to borrow details from other stories; here it is done to create the atmosphere of patriarchal times and there is no suggestion in the story that Tb is intended to be a rewritten patriarchal story brought up to date. It is a matter of simple borrowing of details and is no different from the other borrowings in Tb—of phraseology from elsewhere in the OT and of details from folklore. [54]

The situation in the case of the book of Jonah is not so clear-cut because there are potentially significant relations with two texts: the mention of the prophet Jonah in 2 Kgs 14, 25 and the text of Jer 18, 8 alluded to in Jon 3, 10. But what sort of relation is it? Did the author of Jon merely borrow the name of Jonah from Kgs, as he did details from the stories of Elijah and Elisha and other material from Jer and from folklore, [55] to compose a bit of free haggadah with a didactic purpose, or did the author wish to embellish on 2 Kgs 14, 25 in the manner of GA and write a midrash? Or, is Jon a sermon in story form based

---

54. See D. C. Simpson, "The Book of Tobit," *The Apocrypha and Pseudepigrapha of the Old Testament in English,* ed. R. H. Charles (reprinted ed.; Oxford, 1963) I, 187-94.

55. A. Feuillet, "Les sources du livre de Jonas," *RB* 54 (1947) 161-86.

on Jer 18, 8 ("If that nation concerning which I have spoken turns from evil, I will repent of the evil that I thought to do it") since the Jer text is clearly alluded to in Jon 3, 10? [56]

Surely if Jon were found in a rabbinic midrash after the text of 2 Kgs or Jer there would be no question that it would be a haggadic work applied to Scripture in order to indicate interpretation or to provide illustration or expansion and would truly be a midrash.   But since it is not placed in such a context in the Bible, we must decide if the mere use of the prophet's name or the Jer citation is enough to create that context.   The writer would consider the allusions to 2 Kgs and Jer far too weak to give the impression that Jon is a midrash on either of them.   One would expect a few more allusions to a particular text if the book were intended to be a midrash on that text; also the borrowings from elsewhere in Kgs and from folklore would suggest that the name Jonah and the Jer text are simply borrowings in the same spirit.   In any event, the point we wish to make here is that it is on these grounds that one should determine whether Jon is a midrash or not—and not on the grounds of the fictional or didactic elements, or because Jon "prolongs the doctrine of Jeremiah" as Bloch would have it. [57]

---

56. Thus L. H. Brockington, "Jonah," *Peake's Commentary on the Bible,* eds. M. Black and H. H. Rowley (London, 1962) 627.

57. Bloch, *VDBS* 5, 1275.   If the prolonging of a theme constitutes midrash, then most of the Bible is a midrash for one reason or another, since much of it prolongs the themes of the Pentateuch and it is not uncommon for later biblical writers to take up themes of earlier writers and restate or develop those ideas.   This prolonging of a theme is frequently done in such a way that it focuses the reader's attention on no particular text of the past and therefore there is no justification to classify such literature as midrash.   The prolonging of a theme is something that is found in every genre

SOME HOMILIES

Peder Borgen has isolated in the works of Philo a number of homilies (*De Mutatione nominum* 253-263; *Legum allegoriae* III, 65-75a; 162-168; 169-173; *De sacrificiis Abelis et Caini* 76-87; *De somniis* II, 17-30) which are similar in structure to the homily in Jn 6, 31-58, and he has demonstrated that they are all constructed on a homiletic pattern found in the later Palestinian midrash.[58] The pattern is to begin with a citation of Scripture usually from the Pentateuch (in the homily of Jn 6 it is in v. 31: "he gave them bread from heaven to eat"). This is followed by an exegetical paraphrase of each part of the text in a successive sequence (e.g., first the theme of "he gave them bread from heaven" in Jn 6, 32-48, then the theme "to eat" in Jn 6, 49-58).

---

and is a characteristic that is quite secondary, if indeed it is correct to speak of it as a genre characteristic at all.

K. Budde ("Vermutungen zum 'Midrasch des Buches der Könige,'" *ZAW* 12 [1892] 37-38) has suggested that Jon was originally part of the Midrash of the Book of the Kings mentioned in 2 Chr 24, 27 and that Jon originally stood in relation to 2 Kgs 14, 25 in that work but has since been excerpted and stands alone. The suggestion has found few adherents, for there is no evidence to support the assertion, nor even to support Budde's presuppositions on the nature of the Midrash of the Book of the Kings. In the same vein, H. Winckler (*Altorientalische Forschungen,* 2d series 2 [1899] 260f.) proposes that Jon is a fragment of a midrash on all the prophets, the one called the Chronicles of the Seers in 2 Chr 33, 19; but again the assertion is pure speculation. However, granting for the sake of discussion that Jon once was a midrash because of the context given it, it is not a midrash now because it is no longer in its original context (unless of course one feels that the original context is still preserved by the strength of the allusions to 2 Kgs or Jer).

58. P. Borgen, *Bread From Heaven* (Leiden, 1965) 28-98.

The closing statements refer back to the main statement at the beginning and at the same time sum up points from the homily as a whole. Commonly within the homily there is a subordinate citation (e.g., Jn 6, 45) to which a few lines of commentary are devoted. [59] These pieces discussed by Borgen are fine examples of midrash in homily form, compositions which take a text and apply it or adapt it to contemporary needs. The same homiletic pattern is also observable in Gal 3, 6-29 (on Gn 15, 6) and Rom 4, 1-25 (likewise on Gn 15, 6) and these Pauline passages are examples of midrash too, regardless of whether they are homilies that have been incorporated into the text as Borgen suggests.

Those homilies of the Fathers which set out to comment on biblical texts and which have been influenced directly or through the NT by their Jewish counterparts can also be classified as midrash, and this tradition should be seen as an offshoot of the parent Jewish tradition. [60]

---

59. In Jn 6 the pattern is complete in 6, 31-50 and perhaps this was the original discourse, 51-58 being a later addition. For this and a slightly different treatment of the whole discourse see R. Brown, *The Gospel According to John, I-XII* (New York, 1966) 277-78, 293-94.

60. Cf. Bo Reicke, "A Synopsis of Early Christian Preaching," *The Root of the Vine: Essays in Biblical Theology*, ed. A. Fridrichsen (Westminster, 1953) 128-60; W. B. Sedgwick, "The Origins of the Sermon," *HibbJ* 45 (1946-47) 158-64; art. "Predigt" in *RGG*³ (5, 516-19) and *LTK*² (8, 705-13). Also many of the reworkings and embellishments on the NT Scriptures in the apocryphal material were the Christian midrashic counterpart to Jewish material on the OT. For a discussion of the evidence for the existence of ancient Jewish-Christian exegetical midrashim see J. Daniélou, *The Theology of Jewish Christianity* (Chicago, 1964) 97-107.

However, there are some sermons in the pre-rabbinic literature which are not midrashic. An example would be 4 Mc. The work is a discourse on the supremacy of religious reason over the passions and is a splendid piece of Hellenistic oratory. It has on the one hand been assessed as a synagogue sermon because its reference (1, 10) to the feast being celebrated (Hanukkah?) and its religious tone including the use of doxologies (1, 12; 18, 24) argue strongly for its deliverance in a context of worship. On the other hand it has been classified as a lecture because it has as its point of departure a philosophico-religious thesis and not a biblical text—a departure from the seemingly regular synagogue practice of beginning with a scriptural text. It is true that for the non-biblical point of departure we have no parallel to 4 Mc (save in a sense Heb 11 and Wis 10) but it is doubtful if we know enough about Judeo-Hellenistic practice to judge the question of the synagogal origins of 4 Mc on that basis. It is even possible, as Thyen suggests, [61] that the Scripture text was not part of the homily but was simply the synagogue reading (from 2 Mc?) that preceded. However, regardless of its original *Sitz im Leben,* as 4 Mc stands now (i.e., without that Scripture reading) it is not a midrash because it is not a discourse on a text but on a religious thesis. And the same should be said for the embellishments on 2 Mc contained in the discourse: these could be embellishments in the spirit of GA and LAB but it is not clear from the work that the discourse is to be taken in the context of 2 Mc and it seems better to view the embellishments as existing for oratorical effect to heighten the thesis being discussed.

---

61. H. Thyen, *Der Stil der jüdisch-hellenistischen Homilie* (Göttingen, 1955) 13-14.

THE HOMILY OF WIS 11-19

The structure of this work we have discussed elsewhere. [62]
The composition begins with a brief narrative summing up
the desert journey (Wis 11, 2-4) and then, apropos of the
incident of the water from the rock, a theme is enunciated:
"For by the things through which their foes were punished
they in their need were benefited" (11, 5). This theme
is then illustrated with five antithetical diptychs (11, 6-19,
22) which are punctuated with digressions of various lengths:

Introductory narrative (11, 2-4)
Theme (11, 5)
Illustration of the theme in five diptychs
1. Water from the rock instead of the plague of the
   Nile (11, 6-14)
2. Quail instead of the plague of little animals (11,

---

62. "The Structure of Wisdom 11-19," *CBQ* 27 (1965) 28-34.
There we showed that the beginning of the composition is 11, 2
and not 10, 1, that the theme of the whole composition is 11, 5 and
that the theme is illustrated not by seven antithetical diptychs, as is
frequently stated, but by five. Since then, James M. Reese has pointed
out that many of the sections of Wis have been marked off by the
author with inclusions ("Plan and Structure in the Book of Wisdom,"
CBQ 27 [1965] 391-99). In a recent article in *Bib* (48 [1967] 165-
84) we review the structure of the whole book and show that the
limits of all the sections as well as of the paragraphs within the sections are marked with inclusions. With regard to the major divisions of
the homily of 11-19 we would here reaffirm for the reasons already
stated (*art. cit.*, 32, n. 11) that 16, 5-15 and 18, 20-25 (which have
been set off with inclusions by the author) are digressions and not
diptychs, but it is now clear that the fifth diptych extends from
18, 5 to 19, 22 (inclusions: *laou sou/laon sou* [18, 7 and 19, 22]
and *edoxasas* [18, 8 and 19, 22]) and that 19, 6-21 is a digression
within it (inclusion: *genei/genos* 19, 6 and 21).

15-16, 15; with three digressions: 11, 17-12, 22;
13, 1-15, 17; 16, 5-15)

3. A rain of manna instead of the plague of storms
(16, 16-22; with a digression: 16, 23-29)

4. The pillar of fire instead of the plague of darkness
(17, 1-18, 4)

5. The tenth plague and the exodus by which God
punished the Egyptians and glorified Israel (18,
5-19, 22; with two digressions: 18, 20-25 and
19, 6-21).

The work, then, is structured on the narrative and theme
of 11, 2-5 and resembles very much a homily [63] (regardless
of whether or not it was ever delivered as such). It recalls
for the encouragement of afflicted Jews in Alexandria that
once before Israel had suffered in Egypt and the Lord had
come to their rescue. It spells out in great detail the mar-
velous fidelity and providential workings of the Lord and
in this way attempts to stir up hope for another similar intervention on behalf of the just—perhaps an eschatological
intervention. [64]

The homily is an excellent example of a midrash. It is
true that it is not structured on an explicit citation of a

---

63. The frequent direct address to God whose salvific actions
are being recalled finds a homiletic parallel in 4 Mc where Eleazar
and the Mother, whose actions are there being recalled, are addressed
by the speaker (4 Mc 7, 6-15; 15, 16-20. 29-32; 16, 14ff., etc.).

64. Because of the present juxtaposition of 11-19 to the eschatological chs. 1-6 the intervention of God at the exodus is perhaps being
used as an image of His eschatological intervention. The idea is explicit in 17, 21. See G. Kuhn, "Beiträge zur Erklärung des Buches der
Weisheit," ZNW 28 (1929) 334-41; J. Fichtner, "Die Stellung der
Sapientia Salomonis in der Literatur- und Geistesgeschichte ihrer
Zeit," ZNW 36 (1937) 113-132.

specific text, but this is much too rigid a criterion. The narrative of 11, 2-4 is a digest of Ex 12, 37-17, 7 (somewhat influenced in its formulation by Ps 107, 4-6 which apparently was understood as referring to the exodus) and the author is really calling to mind these chapters of Ex as his point of departure. (The same sort of digest is used as the point of departure for the midrash in Heb 7 [cf. 7, 1-3] and in 1 Cor 10 [cf. 10, 1-5] mentioned below.) After the narrative the author then states the pattern he has detected in comparing those events with the plagues on Egypt in Ex 7-12 and proceeds to help his audience to the same insight. Throughout the discussion there is on the one hand careful attention to the details of the biblical texts and a desire to explain the reasons for happenings (e.g., 11, 7. 8-9. 15-16; 16, 3-4. 6. 11; 18, 5) and to draw out applications for the present (e.g., 16, 23-29; 19, 22), and on the other hand a creative handling of the biblical material: details are altered to fit the purposes of the author, events are idealized and embellished upon with legendary and imaginative material to make them more ample, vivid and edifying (e.g., 11, 4; 16, 2-3. 18. 20; 17, 1-21; 18, 12. 17-19; 19, 7). [65] Because the whole work is structured on 11, 2-4 the whole work is a midrash and not just the embellishments and interpretative remarks. It has been suggested that these chapters at one time constituted

---

65. This aspect is well described by R. Siebeneck, "The Midrash of Wisdom 10-19," *CBQ* 22 (1960) 176-82. For contacts between Wis 11-19 and Jewish midrashic traditions see E. Stein, "Ein jüdisch-hellenistischer Midrasch über den Auszug aus Ägypten," *MGWJ* 78 (1934) 558-75, and G. Camps, "Midraš sobre la història de les plagues," *Miscellanea biblica B. Ubach* (Montserrat, 1953) 97-113.

a Passover Haggadah recited in Egypt, [66] but perhaps there
is more precision in this judgment than one is entitled to
by the evidence.

The homily is not developed on any Jewish homiletic
pattern but in a *synkrisis* (or comparison), and some speak
of *synkrisis* as the genre of Wis 11-19. [67] Even if *synkrisis*
is a genre (it would seem to be simply a technique) and the
work is of a composite genre (synkristic midrash), the
more basic genre is midrash, for even on the level of external
form it is more basic that the diptychs are structured on
11, 2-4 than that the diptychs are antithetical.

Wis 11-19 is a very useful biblical illustration of what
a midrash is. The fact that it is classified as a midrash first
and foremost because it is structured on the biblical paraphrase of 11, 2-4 and is throughout a discussion of the
Ex texts sets in relief the note of "literature about a literature"
as a primary characteristic of the genre. The fact that it
is a homily helps to focus attention on "homiletic actualization
of Scripture" as another basic characteristic. In addition
Wis 11-19 (which as a whole is an example of one form
of midrash, the homily) contains a fine example of another
type of midrash, rewritten Bible or narrative midrash, in
17, 1-21 where it can be pointed out with clarity that fiction
which is midrashic is fiction at the service of the biblical text;

---

66. K. Kohler, "Wisdom of Solomon, Book of the," *The Jewish
Encyclopedia* 12 (New York, 1907) 539.

67. Cf. F. Focke, *Die Entstehung der Weisheit Salomos* (Göttingen, 1913) 12 and the many who follow him. For the classical
use of this figure see F. Focke, "Synkrisis," *Hermes* 58 (1923) 327-
68, and for its use in Jewish literature see Stein, *art. cit.*, and I.
Heinemann, "Synkrisis oder äussere Analogie in der 'Weisheit
Salomos,'" *TZ* 4 (1948) 241-52.

and since this feature is not constant in the work but is quite secondary and can therefore in no way be mistaken as the basic reason for classification, one can easily convey the idea from it that fiction is but one of many techniques used by the genre and is by no means synonymous with the word midrash.

SMALLER MIDRASHIC UNITS

The literary genre midrash is not made up exclusively of works of considerable size and of homogeneous content. Just as in the rabbinic usage of the term midrash a single interpretative statement was called a midrash, so it is legitimate to use the modern literary term in the same way and classify in the genre interpretative units found within works of other genres. For example in CD 4, 12-19 we find the following passage:

> And in all those years (13) Belial shall be unleashed against Israel; as God said by the hand of the prophet Isaiah son of (14) Amoz, *Terror and pit and snare are upon thee, O inhabitant of the land.* The explanation of this [*pišrô*] (is that) (15) these are Belial's three nets, of which Levi son of Jacob spoke, (16) by which he (Belial) ensnared Israel, (17) and which he set [be]fore them as three sorts of righteousness: the first is lust, the second is riches, (and) the third (18) is defilement of the Sanctuary. Whoever escapes this is caught by that, and whoever escapes that one is caught (19) by this.[68]

---

68. The translations of the QL are taken from Dupont-Sommer, *op. cit.* (see n. 12 above).

Here in a description of the years before the consummation
of the end-time we have a citation from Is 24, 17, and following it an interpretation of the text. The author introduces
his interpretation with the word *pišrô,* so that as a result the
section looks like an excerpt from a *pēšer* in form as well
as in method and content. Ll. 14b-19 then constitute a
midrash within a work of another genre. Similar midrashic
units constructed on explicit citations can be found in CD
4, 2-4; 6, 4-11; 7, 12-8, 2; 8, 10-12; 19, 9-14. 22-24; 1QS
8, 15-16; Heb 3, 7-4, 11 (the midrash on Ps 95); Heb 7,
11-28 (on Ps 110, 4); 1 Cor 1, 18-2, 14 (on Is 33, 10.
18; Ps 33, 10); 1 Cor 9, 8-12 (on Dt 25, 4); Eph 4, 8-14
(on Ps 68, 18).

Midrashic units built on implicit citations are found in
Heb 7, 1-10 (on Gn 14, 18-20); [69] Gal 4, 21-31 (on Gn
21, 2-13); 1 Cor 10, 1-13 (on the exodus traditions);
2 Cor 3, 7-18 (on Ex 34, 29-35). In 2 Esd 7, 132-40 the
biblical text (Ex 34, 6) is cited word by word and explained:

> (132) I answered and said, "I know, O Lord, that
> the Most High is now called *merciful,* because he has
> mercy on those who have not yet come into the world;
> (133) and *gracious,* because he is gracious to those who
> turn in repentance to his law; (134) and *patient,* because
> he shows patience toward those who have sinned, since
> they are his own works; (135) and *bountiful,* because he
> would rather give than take away; (136) and *abundant
> in compassion,* because he makes his compassions abound
> more and more to those now living and to those who are
> gone and to those yet to come, (137) for if he did not

---

69. Cf. J. Fitzmyer, " 'Now This Melchizedek . . .' (Heb 7, 1),"
CBQ 24 (1963) 305-21.

make them abound, the world with those who inhabit it would not have life, etc.[70]

Even the brief lines in Sir 7, 27-28 could be considered a midrash on Ex 20, 12, providing motives for the observance of the commandment:

> With your whole heart *honor your father;*
> *your mother*'s birthpangs forget not.
> Remember, of these parents you were born;
> what can you give them for all they gave you?

NON-MIDRASHIC PASSAGES

Mlle. Bloch speaks of meditation and reflection on Scripture, the reworking and citing of texts and especially anthological style as midrash, [71] and the implication seems to be that almost every citation of Scripture, especially if it is multiple, indicates the presence of the literary form midrash, and indeed the citations themselves seem to be viewed as midrash.

There is, of course, a certain element of truth in the idea and this makes it plausible on first sight. Every citation of Scripture contains an implicit exegesis since the citation expresses the author's understanding of the text and sometimes even his exegetical methods. Furthermore, all uses of Sacred Scripture can be seen as a result of meditation and reflection on prior texts. An author's ability to cite presupposes some acquaintance with the material and one can presume that a certain amount of thoughtful consideration has been given to the text prior to its use. Moreover, every

---

70. Cf. D. Simonsen, "Ein Midrasch im IV. Buch Esra," *Festschrift I. Lewy* (Breslau, 1911) 270ff.

71. See above, pp. 19-20.

citation from the Bible is made because the text is seen
as relevant to the topic being discussed; otherwise the citations
would be meaningless. Thus, behind every use of Scripture
there lies interpretation, reflection, and the perception of
relevancy.

However, there are several important distinctions to be
made:

1) A text of Scripture may be cited by an author to
contribute something to a new composition (as in Chr),
or it may be cited so that a new composition may contribute
something by way of understanding to the Scripture text
(GA, the *pešārîm*). The first type of citation may occur
in any literary form (even in midrash, e.g., the secondary
citations in the *pešārîm*) but it does not make a composition
midrash. The work containing the second type of citation
is midrash because of the nature of the composition.

2) Meditation on Scripture can be a *pre-literary process*
which underlies the use of citations in a given work and
makes it possible for the Scripture citations to be used
to full advantage in the new composition; or the *new work
itself* can be a meditation on a biblical text and be written
to lead the reader to insights into that text. Only the latter
is midrash, because only in that case are we concerned with
a composition and, therefore, with a literary form.

3) An author can cite or paraphrase a text and, while
the text is understood in a certain sense (material exegesis),
no emphasis is put on the interpretation and it is assumed
that the reader will concur in the interpretation; or an
author can cite a text in a certain sense and intend by the
way he uses or paraphrases the citation to contribute to an
understanding of that text (formal exegesis). Only the

latter is midrash since only there does the new composition exist for the sake of the text.

Thus, we see that in biblical citations two directions of movement are possible: either a biblical text contributes to the new composition and is for the sake of the new composition or the new composition contributes to an understanding of the text cited and is for the sake of the biblical citation. Only the latter is midrash since only there does the composition actualize Scripture. In the former case (which is mere literary dependence) the author may have put attention on a text and made it relevant in his own mind but he does not write a midrash. He merely uses the results of a previous midrash (written or mental) as he proceeds to write a composition of another genre. [72]

---

72. M. Gertner ("Midrashim in the New Testament," *JSemS* 7 [1962] 267-92) distinguishes only between overt and covert (or invisible) midrash. In the former the text is quoted and the interpretation is given separately and explicitly. The latter is presented either in the form of a concise paraphrase of the text or of an expanded paraphrastic composition. The midrashic nature of the latter is not therefore easily recognized and to establish such a piece of writing as a midrash, Gertner states, one must find the scriptural text involved, the particular notion and meaning of the text contained and established by that interpretation, and the specific hermeneutical technique by which the interpretation has been achieved. To set up these as criteria is to make a midrash out of every paraphrase of a biblical text that can be related to some hermeneutical principle. There is a confusion here between midrash as method and midrash as genre (which Gertner himself senses when he speaks of the covert midrash as being "demidrashized" in its form); three of his four examples of covert midrash (Mk 4, 1-22; Lk 1, 76-79; Jas) are not literary pieces that can be classified as midrash at all, for in their present form Mk 4 and Jas are not in the context of a biblical text and the Lucan selection is better taken as a case in which an OT text is contributing to a new composition (see below,

The following are examples of non-midrashic passages containing Scripture citations. In Sir 48, 9-11 the author cites Mal 3, 23-24 as part of the narrative:

> You [Elias] were taken aloft in a whirlwind,
>   in a chariot with fiery horses.
> You are destined, it is written, in time to come
>   to put an end to wrath *before the day of the Lord,*
> *To turn back the hearts of fathers toward their sons*
>   and to re-establish the tribes of Jacob.
> Blessed are those who saw you, etc.

and in Tb 8, 5-7 a citation from Gn (2, 18) is incorporated:

> And Tobias began to pray,
>   Blessed art thou, O God of our fathers,
>   and blessed be thy holy and glorious name for ever.
>   Let the heavens and all of thy creatures bless thee.
>   Thou madest Adam and gavest him Eve his wife
>   as a helper and support.
>   From them the race of mankind has sprung.
>   Thou didst say, *"It is not good that the man should
>   be alone;*
>   *let us make a helper for him like himself"*
>   And now, O Lord, I am not taking this sister of mine,
>   etc.

---

n. 75). We do not restrict the literary genre midrash to overt midrashim alone and we quite readily admit the covert as a midrashic form (e.g., Sir 7, 27-28 above and CD 20, 17-20; Bar 2, 20-25, etc., below), but we would require that in a paraphrase the allusions to the text be strong enough to set the whole thing in the context of that text for the reader and we would insist on the distinctions in our text above as the more basic criteria for establishing a piece of writing as midrash.

In both of these cases the text is of course cited in a specific sense and thus materially exegeted, but there is no question of the new composition formally exegeting the texts and being written for that purpose. The text is simply contributing something to the new work. (Cf. also the citations in the antitheses of the Sermon on the Mount, Mt 5, 21ff.) And the same is true of many implicit citations; [73] they simply contribute ideas, terminology, authority, etc., to a new literary production:

CD 5, 15-18

> (15) For formerly [also] God visited (16) their works, and His anger was kindled against their forfeits. *For this is a people without understanding* (Is 27, 11); (17)*they are a nation void of counsel* for *there is no understanding among them* (Dt 32, 38). For formerly (18) Moses and Aaron arose by the hand of the prince of lights, etc.

1QS 10, 16-17

> (16) I will confess Him because He is marvelous and will meditate on His might;
> and I will lean on His favors every day.
> I know that *in His hand* is judgment (17) *of all the living* (Jb 12, 10)

---

73. I.e., those without introductory formulae, whether they be virtual citations (exact reproductions of biblical texts with the intent to cite but without the introductory formulae) or allusions. The practice of indicating OT quotations with formal introductions became common only in the latter part of the first century B.C. Hence most of the citations of the OT in the OT are implicit.

and that all His works are truth, etc.
Jb 7, 17-18

What is man, that you make much of him
or pay him any heed?
You observe him with each new day
and try him at every moment.
How long will it be before you look away from me,
and let me alone long enough to swallow my
spittle?

Here a hymnic motif from Ps 8, 4 is changed into a rebellious
statement; the same psalm text apparently also inspired 2 Esd
8, 34-35 where it becomes a call upon God's mercy:

But what is man, that thou art angry with him; or what
is a corruptible race, that thou art so bitter against
it?   For in truth there is no one among those who
have been born who has not acted wickedly, and
among those who have existed there is no one who
has not transgressed.

None of these passages is a midrash.

Likewise a proof or fulfillment text is not of itself a midrash. It is necessary to distinguish between *mere* application of
a text to a new situation and exposition of a text to show *how*
it applies to a new situation.   Only the latter is a composition
and deserving of the name of a literary genre.   Hence the
proof/fulfillment texts in 1 Mc 7, 16-17; 1QM 11, 11-12;
CD 1, 13-14; 6, 11-14; Mt 3, 3; 4, 14-16 and the many
others like them in the QL and the NT are not a midrash
in themselves nor do they make the passage midrashic.   Occasionally, however, there is added to a proof/fulfillment

text an explanation, and such a brief explanation is a midrash (e.g., 1 Cor 15, 56). [74]

Sometimes of course it is difficult to tell in which direction the movement is between text and citation. An example would be CD 8, 14-18:

> (14) But that which Moses said, *Not because of thy righteousness or the uprightness of thy heart art thou going in to inherit* (15) *those nations* (Dt 9, 5a), *but because He loved thy Fathers and because He kept the oath* (Dt 7, 8a), (16) so is it with the converts of Israel (who) have departed from the way of the people; because of God's love for (17) the first who [testified] in His favour He loves those who have followed after, for theirs is the (18) Covenant of the Fathers. But because of His hatred for the builders of the wall His Anger is kindled.

In this passage the author cites the texts and then goes on to say that an analogous situation obtains in his own day. On the one hand, the texts cited may have been merely recalled so that a conclusion might be drawn from them and,

---

74. On the midrashic nature of this text see M. Gertner, *art. cit.*, 282-83.

It is, of course, possible to conceive of the gospels being, in whole or in part, a series of testimonia interspersed with narrative to show fulfillment or Christian interpretation of OT texts, and thus to call a gospel or a part of it a midrash (e.g., J. W. Doeve, "Le rôle de la tradition orale dans la composition des évangiles synoptiques," *La formation des évangiles,* éds., J. Cambier et L. Cerfaux [Bruges, 1957] 70-84; F. F. Bruce, "The Book of Zechariah and the Passion Narrative," *BJRylL* 43 [1960-61] 336-53). But this raises the very real question if testimonia plus narrative and Christian interpretation is an adequate description of the gospel material.

thus, are merely contributing data for the new composition. On the other hand, the piece could be understood as an application of the ancient text to a new situation followed by a midrashic attempt (lines 16--18) to bring out the message that the text should have for the sect.

In 1QS 2, 2-4 it is again difficult to decide in which direction the movement lies between citation and composition:

> And the priests shall bless all (2) the men of the lot of
> God who walk perfectly in all His ways, and shall say:
> May He bless thee *with all* (3) *goodness,*
>   and keep thee *from all evil*
> May He enlighten *thy heart with understanding of life,*
>   and favor thee *with everlasting knowledge.*
> (4) May He lift His *gracious* face towards thee
>   to grant thee *eternal* bliss.

Here, in a description of the ceremony of entry into the community, we find an embellishment (given above in italics) on the Aaronic blessing of Nm 6, 24-26.   In a sense the additions are interpretative [75] and the new composition could

---

75. Thus Brownlee, *art. cit.* (see n. 6), 60, and Gertner, *art. cit.* (see n. 72) 277.—Gertner points out that the seven concepts of the Aaronic blessing are contained in the *Benedictus* (blessing [v. 68]; keeping [save and deliver in vv. 71 and 74]; face [vv. 75. 76]; ḥnn [give v. 77; mercy v. 78]; lifting [= forgive v. 77]; shining [v. 79]; peace [v. 79].   He suggests that the first part (vv. 68-75) is a psalmistic poem based on the blessing and that the last part (vv. 76-79) is a covert midrash on the blessing in the form of a paraphrase shaped as a liturgical piece.   Since the seven concepts are distributed through both parts, it is hard to see why both parts are not simply a poem based on the blessing.   Gertner himself says that the only clue to the midrashic nature of 76-79 is its differing in style and structure from the poem.   This simply means it is an addition, not a midrash.

be seen as a midrash to expand the old text and bring out its implications. It is, however, possible (and much more plausible to the present writer) that the new composition does not exist for the sake of the text but for the sake of a liturgy, and that both Nm 6 and the author (and Ps 121) have contributed something to the formula.[76] This is clearly the case in 1QS 2, 8-9 where the same Aaronic blessing is turned into a curse against the men of the lot of Belial:

> May God not favor thee when thou callest upon Him
> and may He be without forgiveness to expiate thy sins.
> May He lift His angry face to revenge Himself upon thee,
> and may there be for thee no (word) of peace
> on the lips of all who cling (to the Covenant) of the Fathers.

and in 1QS 2, 12-18 where Dt 29, 18-20 provides the wording.

Again, Sirach takes Prv 11, 4a

> Wealth (*hôn*) is useless on the day of wrath

and expands it to

> Do not rely on deceitful wealth (*nksy šqr*)
> for it will be useless on the day of wrath (Sir 5, 10).

Perhaps it is an attempt to elucidate the proverb and to bring out the full meaning of "wealth" in Prv as Ben Sira understood it, or perhaps Ben Sira merely took the proverb and used it for his own purposes without intending to focus attention on the original text. Only the former would be midrash.

Sirach also takes Prv 12, 9

---

76. In the same way Nm 6 has contributed to Ps 67 and 121.

Better a lowly man who has a servant (*w'bd lw*)
than the boaster who is without bread

and restates it thus:

Better the worker who has plenty of everything
than the boaster who is without sustenance (Sir 10,
26).

Here there is the added difficulty of an ambiguous consonantal
text in Prv.   The phrase *w'bd lw* can be translated "who has
a servant" (thus MT) or as "and works for himself" (thus 1
MS, LXX and Syr).   Ben Sira could be merely borrowing
from the proverb or he could be explicitly interpreting in a
midrash either of the above readings—and perhaps precisely
in order to eliminate the ambiguity.

ANTHOLOGICAL   STYLE

Anthological style, in the words of André Robert, "con-
siste à réemployer, littéralement ou équivalemment, les mots
ou formules des Écritures antérieures." [77]   It is of course
well known that this process was frequently used in the postexilic period in the canonical and non-canonical literature.
The postexilic period brought new problems and needs, and
the responses to these needs were sought in the Scriptures.
This seeking in and meditating on the Bible often resulted
in new works which would take up expressions and ideas of
predecessors, develop, enrich and transpose the earlier message and thus pass to a new stage of thought while still speaking in the language of the ancients.

Bloch and Robert and subsequently others have equated
anthological style with midrash. [78]   They see in it the two

---

77. A. Robert, "Littéraires (genres)," *VDBS* 5, 411.
78. See Introduction, nn. 9 and 24.

basic characteristics of the midrashic genre: meditation on Scripture and actualization of Scripture for contemporary needs. From our remarks above it should be clear that such an automatic equation of anthological style with the literary form midrash is not valid. As with single citations, so also with multiple ones there are two possible directions of movement between a citation and the new work in which it is found. Only if the audience's attention is focused on the prior text and if the new composition exists for the sake of the old text can the work be called a midrash. The borrowing, adaptation and transformation of older material in such a way that the older material merely contributes to the new work as a source is not midrashic. Moreover, anthological style can be a process resorted to merely out of a desire to speak in the language of the Bible for one reason or another, and this can hardly be conceived of as an attempt to make earlier Scripture relevant for a later age. Thus, in discussing the possibility of midrash in a given passage, one has not exhausted the question when one establishes the anthological character of the passage, but one must then carry the investigation further to see whether the anthology is a sign of mere literary dependence or an indication that texts are being cited in order to contribute some understanding to them.

The *Benedictus*, [79] the *Magnificat* [80] and 1QM 12 [81] are

---

79. See A. Plummer, *A Critical and Exegetical Commentary on the Gospel According to S. Luke* (*ICC;* Edinburgh, [5]1922) 39.

80. *Ibid.,* 30-31, and R. Laurentin, *Structure et théologie de Luc I-II* (Paris, 1957) 82-85.

81. For the textual analysis see J. Carmignac, "Les Citations de l'ancien testament dans 'La Guerre des fils de lumière contre les fils de ténèbres,'" *RB* 63 (1956) 254-60; *id., La Règle de la guerre* (Paris, 1958) 171-87.

good examples of non-midrashic anthology. All three are a veritable mosaic of biblical citations and by no stretch of the imagination could they be conceived of as in any way being written for the benefit of the original texts or even of some of the texts. Not only the number of texts cited but also, and especially, the way they are cited clearly indicates that it is a case of prior texts serving as a source and providing terminology and atmosphere for a new work.

Examples of midrashic anthological style are difficult to find but perhaps CD 20, 17-20 could be so classified:

> (17) . . . But *those who are converted from the sin of J[a]c[ob]* (Is 59, 20), who have kept the Covenant of God, *they will then speak one* (18) *with another* (Mal 3, 16) to justify each man his brother by supporting their steps in the way of God. *And God will heed* (19) their words *and will hear, and a reminder will be written [before Him] of them that fear God and of them that revere* (20) *His name* (Mal 3, 16), *until salvation and justice are revealed* to them that fear [God] (Is 56, 1?). *[And] you will distinguish anew between the just* (21) *and the wicked between him that has served God and him that has served Him not* (Mal 3, 18). *And He will be merciful to [thousands]* (Ex 20, 6) *to them that love Him, for a thousand generations* (Dt 7, 9).

The passage first of all identifies the *šby pš'* of Is 59, 20 with those "who have kept the Covenant of God" (the sect). It then goes on to identify the sect with the "they," "them that fear God," and the "you" in Mal 3, 16. 18 (which is apparently seen as a prophetic text). If the allusion to Is 56, 1 is intended, then the text also states that the sect will be the

recipient of the promises of Is 56, 1.   The repetition of the
phrase "them that fear God" in line 20 supports this interpretation of the use of the Isaian quotation.   The subsequent
citations from Ex and Dt merely contribute to the new composition.   They may have been understood as referring to
the sect but CD does not point up that aspect.   It merely
cites them in a certain sense and uses them for what they can
contribute to the work.

Perhaps another example of the midrashic use of anthological style is found in Bar 2, 20-25:

For thou hast sent thy *anger* and	(Jer 36, 7)
thy wrath upon us, as thou didst declare by thy servants the proph- ets, saying: "Thus says the Lord: *Bend your shoulders and serve the*	
king of Babylon, and you will	(Jer 27, 11. 12)
remain in the land which I gave to your fathers. But if you will not obey the voice of the Lord and will not serve the king of Babylon, *I*	(Jer 7, 34; 16, 9;
will make to cease from the cities	33, 11)
of Judah and from the region about Jerusalem the voice of mirth and the voice of gladness, the voice of the bridegroom and the voice of	
the bride, and the whole *land will*	(Jer 33, 10)
be a desolation without inhabi- tants." But we did not obey thy voice, to serve the king of Babylon; and thou hast confirmed thy words, which thou didst speak by thy serv-	
ants the prophets, that *the bones* of	(Jer 8, 1)

our *kings* and the bones of our
fathers *would be brought out of
their graves;* and behold they have
been cast out *to the heat of day
and the frost of night.* They per-   (Jer 36, 30)
ished in great misery *by famine and
sword and pestilence.*   (Jer 14, 12; 38, 2)

In this passage if our analysis is correct, it is not a question
of texts simply being applied to a new situation as in the case
of a proof/fulfillment text, nor is it a question of texts
supplying vocabulary and ideas. Rather, there is here an
arrangement of textual elements from a single chosen biblical
author to apply them to a new (or fulfillment) situation, and
the arrangement then provides us with a composition which
explains how the biblical texts apply to the new situation, thus
accomplishing implicitly what, for example, the midrash in
1 Cor 15, 56 does for its text explicitly. Similar midrashic
passages can be found in Bar 2, 27-35 and Dn 9, 1-19; also
Is 60-62 can be seen as a reinterpretation of the oracles of
Deutero-Isaiah. [82]

It could perhaps be argued that Wis 3-4 should be classified as a midrash because of its anthological style. The first
six chapters of the book are structured as follows: [83]

    a. Exhortation to justice (1, 1-15)
    b. The wicked invite death (speech of the wicked and

---

82. For a compendium of the prophetic material which Trito-
Isaiah took over and actualized and a discussion of the alterations
which he made see W. Zimmerli, "Zur Sprache Tritojesajas," *Sch-
weizerische Theologische Umschau* 20 (1950) 110-22.

83. See A. Wright, "The Structure of the Book of Wisdom,"
Bib 48 (1967) 165-84.

author's comment) (1, 16-2, 24)
c. The hidden counsels of God (3, 1-4, 20)
  1. On suffering (3, 1-12)
  2. On childlessness (3, 13-4, 6)
  3. On early death (4, 7-20)
b'. The final judgment (speech of the wicked and author's comment) (5, 1-23)
a'. Exhortation to seek wisdom (6, 1-21)

In the central section the author gives the "hidden counsels of God" (2, 22) on the three topics central to the Jewish thought on retribution. His teaching is the fruit of meditation on Is 52-66 in its LXX form and he sets forth that teaching in a series of characters or types taken from Is, presented in their Isaian sequence and embellished with additional details from elsewhere. [84] In 3, 2ff. the author is drawing on Is 53, 4-11 on the subject of suffering. In 3, 13ff. he has moved on to Is 54, 1ff. and 56, 2-5 and the subject of childlessness, and in 4, 7ff. he has moved on to Is 57, 1-2 and the subject of early death. The Isaian texts, originally referring to Jerusalem, are thus by implicit citation recalled and are reinterpreted and transferred to the individual order with the help of other implicit citations from Is and elsewhere. The significant thing here is that in the midst of the anthology there are principal texts cited in their Isaian order, so that as a result the central section could be viewed as a midrash on these texts accomplished by an anthological presentation. However, the sequential dependency on Is really begins in 2, 13 (with Is 52, 13) and

---

84. Cf. P. W. Skehan, "Isaias and the Teaching of the Book of Wisdom," *CBQ* 2 (1940) 389-99; M. J. Suggs, "Wisdom of Solomon 2¹⁰ — 5: A Homily Based on the Fourth Servant Song," *JBL* 76 (1957) 26-33.

ends in 5, 22 (with Is 55, 19) and therefore cuts across
the structure which the author has given his material.   This
would seem to indicate that the author is not concerned with
interpreting specific texts in the central section, but that in
chs. 1-6 he is presenting a doctrine and citing the Isaian
material as a source of images for that presentation and by
way of appeal to the authority of that earlier book, as, for
example, he does again with Is, Dt, Hos, Jer and Pss in chs.
13-15 on idolatry.   This would not be midrash.

Another use of anthological style is found in Prv 1-9.
As Robert has pointed out [85] the author of Prv 1-9 has
reused words and phrases of earlier biblical books (Dt, Jer,
and Deutero-Isaiah especially) in order to present wisdom
in the garb of a prophet, in order to identify wisdom in
some way with God, and also, although not in the explicit
manner of Ben Sira and Baruch, to identify wisdom with the
Torah, and to make the ḥăkāmîm heirs of the prophets.   By
such a presentation the author of Prv 1-9 apparently wished
to further incorporate into Judaism a wisdom tradition which
was of foreign and secular origins, and to present wisdom as a
legitimate vehicle for describing the good life under the
Law.   The method which the author of Prv 1-9 used to
accomplish this was the method of allusions.   He does not
cite earlier texts properly speaking or juxtapose texts, but
he employs images and phrases associated with the Torah
and the prophets and uses them in connection with wisdom
to show that the wisdom tradition is the modern counterpart
of ancient realities.

Allusive theology of this sort is not midrashic as Bloch
has suggested. [86]   Specific texts of earlier Scripture are not

---

85. See Introduction, n. 24.
86. *VDBS* 5, 1273.

cited as a point of departure for a discussion that attempts to make these texts relevant for a new generation.   Rather, images and vocabulary strongly associated with the Law and the prophets are now associated with wisdom, and the implication is thus made that there is a continuity between them, and that wisdom is the successor of the prophet and the equivalent of the Law.   There is no attempt to make earlier texts refer to wisdom.   Rather, the earlier texts bestow the Deuteronomic and prophetic mantle upon wisdom personified.   And this is not midrash. [87]

Another variety of this allusive use of anthological style is found in 1QS 8, 4-10.   Unlike Prv 1-9 where it is a question merely of the employment of vocabulary that is associated with institutions of the past, here specific texts are alluded to:

(4)... When these things come to pass in Israel, (5) the Council of the Community shall be established in truth as an everlasting *planting* (Is 60, 21).   It is the house

---

87. G. W. Buchanan's attempt to describe Prv 2, 20-7, 3 as a midrash on Dt 11, 18-22 ("Midrashim pré-tannaïtes.   A propos de Prov., i-ix," *RB* 72 [1965] 227-39) is not convincing.   In addition to the allusions to Dt in Prv 2-7 one must take into account the allusions in these chapters to Jer and Deutero-Isaiah in order to evaluate properly the use of the Deuteronomic vocabulary.   Moreover, the author of Prv 2-7 has not structured his material according to the themes in the Dt text as Buchanan supposes but almost certainly on quite another plan (cf. P. W. Skehan, "The Seven Columns of Wisdom's House in Proverbs 1-9," *CBQ* 9 [1947] 190-98).   Nor are any of the units within Prv 2-7 a midrash. The one text for which a case could seemingly be made and which Buchanan emphasizes is 6, 21-22, and apparently 6, 22 is out of place and should follow 5, 19 (cf. Skehan, "Proverbs 5:15-19 and 6:20-24," *CBQ* 8 [1946] 290-97; CCD; and R. B. Y. Scott, *Proverbs, Ecclesiastes* [New York, 1965] 55, 58).

of holiness for Israel and the Company of infinite (6)
holiness for Aaron; they are the witnesses of truth unto
judgment and the *chosen of loving-kindness* (Is 42, 1
perhaps) appointed to offer expiation for the earth and
to *bring down* (7) *punishments* upon the wicked (Ps
94, 2 perhaps). It is the *tried* wall, the *precious cornerstone;* (8) its *foundations* shall not tremble nor *flee* from
their place (Is 28, 16). It is the Dwelling of infinite
holiness (9) for Aaron in [eternal] knowledge unto the
Covenant of justice. . . .

In lines 7 and 8 there is clearly an allusion to Is 28, 16: the
community is the cornerstone of which Isaiah spoke. In line
5 we have an allusion to the "planting" of Is 60, 21. Of
itself the occurrence of *mt't* here does not necessarily suggest
the Isaian passage, but the term is used elsewhere to designate
the sect (1QS 11, 8; CD 1, 7) and, thus, was apparently a
popular term, and in 1QH 6, 15 and 1QH 8 the connection
is clearly made with Is 60, 21. In line 6 the *bḥyry rswn*
may have been inspired by Is 42, 1: *bḥyry rsth npšy*. If so,
it too would be an allusion by which the community is identified with the Servant of Yahweh who is "appointed to offer
expiation for the earth." This passage could be considered
a midrash (a pointing out of the fulfillment of the respective
prophecies) but the anthological technique does seem to be
of the sort found in Prv 1-9, and perhaps the passage is
better conceived of not as a literature about a literature
(midrash) but as literature about the sect in which Scripture
is used in an allusive manner to interpret the significance of
the community.

It is perhaps in this connection that the genre of Jdt
should be discussed. As Patrick Skehan has pointed out,
the Book of Judith is based in an extraordinary way on Ex,

perhaps on Ex 14, 31 if one were to single out a particular verse. [88]   The Canticle of Judith echoes the Canticle of Miriam and the narrative portion of Jdt reflects primarily the exodus events, so that both in the prose and the poetry what is done by Judith's hand is set forth as a revival of what was done by the hand of God and the hand of Moses at the exodus.

These findings raise anew the question of the literary form of Jdt. Is the book a midrash on Ex 14, 31 (the hand of God in Ex is ever active)?   Or is it an example of allegorical haggadah, a meditation on God's providence and another example of the allusive category of anthological style (the ideal event described in Jdt being equated or likened to the exodus event)?   It is very difficult to decide. If Jdt were found in a Jewish midrashic work after Ex 14, 31, it would clearly be a midrash and a very beautiful one. But are the allusions to Ex strong enough to create that context on their own?   The allusions when perceived are striking, but they are not immediately recognizable nor are they the only allusions to Israel's history, and the repeated idea that as long as Israel does not sin against God it will prosper (4, 12-21; 8, 18-20; 11, 10; 16, 15) suggests that perhaps this was the point of the work in the mind of the author; in this case he did not write a midrash.

One final passage should be mentioned, not so much for its own sake but because it has been so emphasized by Bloch [89]—the allegory of Ez 16.   She points out the many

---

88. "The Hand of Judith," *CBQ* 25 (1963) 94-110.
89. R. Bloch, "Ézéchiel XVI: exemple parfait du procédé midrashique dans la Bible," *Cahiers Sioniens* 9 (1955) 193-223.   Within the article (p. 216) she speaks of Ez 16 belonging to the midrashic genre, a term that she evidently equates with midrash (see Introd., n. 16).

similarities of thought between Ez 16 and Hos (2; 8, 1-9, 10), Jer (3; 12, 7-17) and Dt (4, 1-31; 8, 11-20; 32), and concludes that these earlier texts were reused anthologically, and in this manner were completed and clarified one by the other and transposed to highlight certain points in the sources for the needs of a later generation. Thus the passage, according to Bloch, would be similar to the midrashic examples of anthological style pointed out above. But the fact of the matter is that the passage is not an example of anthological style (i.e., the use, literally or equivalently, of words or formulae of earlier Scripture). It is really an anthology of ideas and images culled from some [90] of the texts mentioned, plus a good deal of originality. No text is cited; in many cases it is not clear exactly which earlier text has provided the image, and a large number of the details of all of the previous texts involved are in no way taken up. Without entering into a detailed discussion of these points here, [91] let us simply remark that once Hosea and Jeremiah uttered their oracles on Israel the faithless wife, anyone who later simply takes up that image to exploit it literarily is not thereby exegeting and actualizing Hos and Jer. Now, if Ezekiel were to exploit the ideas of Hos and Jer in this

---

90. That Dt 4 and 8 provided the background could probably be denied.

91. To say nothing of the probability that Ez 16, 16-21. 26-34. 44-63 are later additions to the allegory to update its application (see the commentaries of Eichrodt, Fohrer and Zimmerli *ad loc.*), something that Bloch does not take into consideration in her discussion of the chapter. W. A. Irwin (*The Problem of Ezekiel* [Chicago, 1943]) and E. Vogt ("Textumdeutungen im Buch Ezechiel," *Sacra Pagina* [Paris, 1959] I, 475-78) speak of such additions in Ez as midrashic, but this is not a correct evaluation (see below on redaction and glosses).

way, it is hard to see how such an effort would differ from what we have in Ez 16; and before affirming that Ezekiel was commenting on or updating Hos and Jer, one would like to see a good deal more concern for the details of the earlier texts (in whatever form Ezekiel knew them). Ez 16 is not a midrash, but it does provide the opportunity to enunciate the principle that the reworking of ideas found in earlier literature does not necessarily produce a midrash. [92]

REDACTION AND GLOSSES

Geza Vermes writes:

The final redaction of the Pentateuch, performed in the spirit of the most recent revision, affected, therefore, the significance of the older material, and established the meaning of the compilation as a whole according to the then contemporary understanding of biblical history. This implicit harmonization and interweaving of scriptural tradition may be termed biblical midrash or haggadah. [93]

And Vermes illustrates these remarks with a discussion of the story of Balaam and shows how P's supplement to

---

92. The same sort of non-midrashic reworking of ideas is operative in the anthological style of Mi 4-5. Cf. B. Renaud, *Structure et attaches littéraires de Michée IV-V* (Paris, 1964), who, however, classifies the chapters as midrash. — The Canticle of Canticles has been termed a midrash because of the allegorical character it supposedly possesses from the alleged anthological process used in its composition (Bloch, *VDBS* 5, 1273, based on the works of Robert and Feuillet on Ct). The arguments for the existence of *style anthologique* in Ct are extremely tenuous (cf. R. E. Murphy, "Recent Literature on the Canticle of Canticles," *CBQ* 16 [1954] 5-8).

93. Vermes, *op. cit.* (see n. 37), 176.

the Balaam story puts a pejorative interpretation on the story and makes Balaam a villain. Pfeiffer calls later explanatory and interpretative additions to Jos and Sm midrash, [94] and Camps suggests that similar additions in Jgs and Kgs are midrash. [95] In the same vein Bloch proposes that glosses are midrash. [96]

The equation of redaction with midrash is nothing else than the logical result of the confusion of method with literary form, and it clearly demonstrates the error of such a confusion. There is a vast difference between the stages in the composition of a book and a commentary upon that book, between the adapting and interpreting of material

---

94. Pfeiffer, *Introduction* . . . , 309, 361, 368-73.

95. Camps, *art. cit.* (see n. 65), 98 n. — Samuel Sandmel ("The Haggadah Within Scripture," *JBL* 80 [1961] 105-22) sees the doublets in Gn, Ex, Jgs, and Sm, not as variant traditions, but as examples of midrash: one story is the primitive version, the other a midrashic retelling of it in the manner of GA. Thus, Gn 20 is a midrash on Gn 12, 9ff.; Gn 15 expands Gn 12, 1; Gn 21, 8-21 is a retelling of Gn 16; 1 Sm 24 is a midrash on 1 Sm 26, etc. As Sandmel remarks: "Were we to find this story [Gn 20] in Genesis Rabbah instead of Gn 20, we would promptly recognize it as a haggadah based on Gn 12, 9ff." (p. 111). According to Sandmel we are not dealing with sources blended but with successive haggadic recastings of a single source. Bit by bit over the years embellishments have been added on to the primitive narrative, neutralizing, correcting and interpreting what was aleady present. Thus, the Abraham of Gn 20 determines and clarifies the character of the Abraham of Gn 12, etc. It may be that some of the doublets were *used* in this manner by the various redactors, but as a systematic solution to the problem of the *origin* of the Pentateuchal material it is an impossible one. Cf. ideas similar to Sandmel's in J. Weingreen, "Exposition in the Old Testament and in Rabbinical Literature," *Promise and Fulfilment*, ed. F. F. Bruce (Edinburgh, 1963) 187-201.

96. *VDBS* 5, 1276.

and a composition that adapts and interprets another composition. The first is a method that can be used in many
literary operations (to assemble oral material into various
literary forms, to put out new editions of such a book, or
to write a new work commenting on a former one). The
second is a literary work with a specific literary form, and
the fact that it uses a certain method does not necessarily
allow one to classify under that literary genre other works
that utilize the same method.

As Mlle. Bloch rightly notes, the gradual fixing of the
sacred text in the postexilic period was of the greatest importance for the birth of the midrashic genre. [97]   Prior to this
period of fixation Israel felt free to re-edit her sacred traditions and to add to them and in this way make them relevant to the needs of the community at that time and to bring
the traditions into accord with developed religious practices.
Once, however, the sacred text was looked upon as un-
alterable, successive editions were no longer possible, and
yet, the need to bridge the gap between the sacred literature
of the past and the needs of the present still remained.
Thus it was that a separate literature grew up—the midrashic
literature—which accomplished by means of works distinct
from the Scriptures being commented upon what redaction
had accomplished during the period of textual fluidity. There
is an organic bond between the redaction of the OT and the
early midrash (and this, of course, is what Bloch, Vermes,
et al., are at pains to point out), but we should not attempt
to express this organic relation by means of literary genres,
grouping under one genre both those works which are the
result of several editions and the later interpretative works,
solely because both the editing and the later works were

---

97. *Ibid.,* 1268.

interpretative. The interpretative works belong to the literary genre midrash; the final redaction of the Pentateuch (to take an example) still belongs to the same genres (sacred history and pre-history, Torah, etc.) as did the earlier redactions.

For this reason glosses strictly speaking should not be classed as midrash. They are really successive additions (albeit often interpretative and at times even characteristic of certain types of rabbinic midrashic exposition [98]) to a book which intentionally or accidentally have become part of that book and are absorbed by the literary form of that book. They do not constitute a literary work separate from the text commented upon.

APOCALYPTIC AND MIDRASH

Renée Bloch has stated that there is a very close relationship between apocalyptic and midrash. She first of all points out the similarities between the two: both literary forms instruct and edify; they hark back to Scripture or oral traditions to reinterpret the past for the sake of the present and the future; both manifest a deep sense of the supernatural and are characterized by hyperbolic style. The difference between the two is that midrash is a work of reflection on traditions and therefore is oriented toward the past, whereas apocalyptic is concerned with revelations and is oriented toward the eschatological future. This difference, though, is only apparent because in reality midrash is concerned with the past for the sake of present and future needs,

---

98. Cf. J. Weingreen, "Rabbinic-Type Glosses in the Old Testament," *JSemS* 2 (1957) 149-62, who, however, does not call them midrash.

and apocalyptic, in order to justify its eschatological predictions, scrutinizes the history of the past or recounts some
alleged prophecy of the past.   Bloch then concludes that
apocalyptic is really only a variety of midrash. [99]   Needless
to say, this discussion of the two literary forms is not a very
satisfying one to the writer.

It is apparently more difficult to isolate the primary
characteristics of apocalyptic than of midrash, [100] but for
our purposes a general descriptive definition of apocalyptic
should suffice.   Apocalyptic is prophecy about the imminent
eschatological future.   In its pure form (i.e., without true
prophetic vision behind it) it presents itself in the guise
of revelations which were allegedly given to some personality
of the past and which have been hidden for a long time and
are now published.   It is frequently characterized by lush
imagery (because it is dealing with the distant future) and
mysterious symbols (because it was often "resistance literature" and it had of necessity to be cryptic).   It is a literature
whose purpose is to stir up hope during days of crisis by
demonstrating that things will get better soon (and hence
there is a fondness for the calculation of times, etc.).   To
establish confidence in this demonstration, something of the
past is set forth and interpreted in order to give credence to
what is said about the future.   It is at this point that we come
to the area where apocalyptic and midrash may be com-
bined in a given work.   If the apocalyptic work scrutinizes
past history for a key to the future, it is simple apocalyptic.

---

99. *VDBS* 5, 1276-78.   Similarly Robert who, however, states
that the two forms are distinct but that sometimes the distinction
is difficult to make in practice (*Guide to the Bible*, I, 509).

100. Cf. B. Vawter, "Apocalyptic: Its Relation to Prophecy,"
CBQ 22 (1960) 33-46 and the bibliography there.

But if the apocalyptic work scrutinizes biblical texts from the past for the answers to the future and reinterprets these texts in the manner proper to apocalyptic, then the work is of a composite genre; it is both apocalyptic and midrash. As always, the factor that determines if midrash is present or not is whether or not the discussion is for the sake of some biblical text; and the deficiencies of the discussion of Bloch on apocalyptic and midrash are that she has introduced into the discussion other characteristics which are not constitutive of midrash and which, as a matter of fact, are secondary characteristics of many literary forms. In conclusion, then, apocalyptic and midrash are distinct literary forms, but sometimes they exist together as a compound literary form when apocalyptic is scrutinizing a text of the past (or conversely, when midrash is interpreting a text in an apocalyptic manner).

To illustrate the above remarks from Dn: Dn 1-6 contains stories about Daniel, a hero of the past. The stories are recounted to attribute the subsequent visions of the book to Daniel and thus give them some authority. The stories also of themselves set forth Daniel as a model of perseverance in adversity and thus encourage the reader in time of persecution. There is nothing midrashic here—although sometimes these stories are called the midrashic section of the book (along with chs. 13-14) because they are didactic fiction; [101] but the remarks made above in the case of Est and Tb are valid here also: the genre is not midrash but haggadah, at the service of apocalyptic. Dn 7-8 are visions allegedly received by Daniel. These chapters are simple apocalyptic, scrutinizing the history of the past and imposing a pattern

---

101. E.g., J. McKenzie, *Dictionary of the Bible* (Milwaukee, 1965) 575; Ellis, *op. cit.* (see n. 45), 451, 517-23; etc.

upon it which indicates that deliverance is at hand. Dn 9, however, is apocalyptic and midrash. Daniel seeks an understanding of the 70 years in the prophecy of Jer (25, 11; 29, 10), and the interpretation of Jer is presented in an apocalyptic manner—an alleged vision and revelation (Dn 9, 20-27). This is the midrashic section in Dn, and not cc. 1-6; 13-14.

Another example of midrashic apocalyptic is 4 Esd 12, 10ff. where the vision and its interpretation in Dn 7 is reinterpreted apocalyptically with alleged revelation. Possibly Ez 38-39 is a midrashic apocalypse, if it is an attempt to reinterpret eschatologically the "foe from the north" in Jer 1, 14; 4, 6; 6, 1. In the NT, the anthological style of Ap, however, is of the non-midrashic variety. [102]

---

102. A work which offers difficulties in the discussion of both apocalyptic and midrash is the Book of Jubilees. The question of the literary form of Jub is a complex one, for it is a book of composite genre: history (in the ancient sense), apocalyptic (it makes Moses the recipient of disclosures on the pattern of history), testament (the several spiritual testaments of the patriarchs) and perhaps midrash (the large amount of embellishments which may be for the sake of the biblical text). One need only look at the various titles the book has been given to see the difficulty involved in ascertaining the literary form: Jubilees, The Little Genesis, Apocalypse of Moses, Testament of Moses, etc. To the present writer apocalyptic seems to be a primary dimension of the work. Jub purports to be a revelation given to Moses and handed down secretly about the fixed pattern of history and its periods. The first period is set forth with a fixed numerical pattern. The second period, in which the author lived, is not recounted or provided with a numerical pattern, but it is described in a summary manner, and it is hinted, undoubtedly to offer encouragement and hope, that the present sufferings are to be interpreted as the tribulations that mark the end of the second period and usher in the third. The primary purpose of retelling the biblical story up to the exodus

ARE THE INFANCY NARRATIVES MIDRASH?

The infancy narrative of Lk has been classified as midrash because of its anthological style, [103] and the narrative of Mt as midrash for various reasons: because it is a development on OT texts, [104] because it is a commentary on OT

---

seems not to have been that of GA, namely, to give a vivid and trouble-free version of Gn, but rather to impose the schematized chronology on Gn, to indicate that the author possessed a knowledge of the rhythm and order of past history, and thereby to reinforce the apocalyptic section (23, 9-32) and inspire confidence in its suggestions that it was the Messianic woes which had arrived.

So much for the apocalyptic nature. Is the work also midrashic since in the course of retelling the biblical narrative much legendary material has been incorporated? On the one hand the work is presented as material given to Moses in addition to what is contained in the Bible; it is presented as a separate and independent work containing the secret pattern of history and could thus be understood as an interpretation of history. On the other hand the work is obviously based on the biblical text and in the re-telling, difficulties in the biblical narrative are solved, gaps supplied, offensive elements removed and the spirit of later Judaism infused into the primitive history. This would suggest that the author had a midrashic aim as well as an apocalyptic one. There is no compelling reason that would prevent us from looking upon the embellishments as midrashic and we would be inclined to see Jub as another example of an apocalyptic-midrashic work.

103 Bloch, *VDBS* 5, 1279; *id.*, "Écriture et tradition dans le Judaïsme," *Cahiers Sioniens* 8 (1954) 31; Laurentin, *op. cit.* (see n. 80) 95, 116-19; R. Dillon, "St. Luke's Infancy Account," *The Dunwoodie Review* 1 (1961) 5-37; McKenzie, *op. cit.*, 575.

104. Bloch, *VDBS* 5, 1279; *id.*, "Écriture...," 31; Laurentin, *op. cit.*, 100-1. What they mean by "development" is not clear: perhaps a semi-fictional piece taking its inspiration from details in the OT text, perhaps a construction of episodes upon texts with no implication as to history or fiction.

texts, [105] because of Mt's dependence on midrashic traditions, the presence of elements apparently legendary and the construction of five episodes on five texts with the referring of OT Scripture to Jesus in whom they are fulfilled. [106]

Of course, neither the fiction nor the anthological style of itself makes these narratives midrash, nor does the fact that allusions are made to midrashic material. The fundamental question is: do the narratives under discussion actualize biblical texts? It is hard to see how the infancy narrative of Lk does. It does not exist for the sake of the many biblical texts alluded to; rather it is concerned with interpreting the Christ-event by means of OT analogies (the same sort of thing that is done by the heavy overlay of OT allusions in the Baptism, Temptation and Transfiguration narratives), and the anthological style is of the non-midrashic variety that we have seen, for example, in 1QS 8, 4-10.

Mt's narrative could be called a midrash if one sees the five texts in the five episodes as the primary point of interest in the narrative. Viewed in this way each episode would be a commentary worked up primarily to show the fulfillment of the text contained within it. But in fact are the OT citations the primary point of interest? They are no different from other fulfillment texts in Mt and the rest

---

105. A. H. McNeile, *The Gospel According to St. Matthew* (London, 1915) 23; G. H. Box, "The Gospel Narratives of the Nativity and the Alleged Influence of Heathen Ideas," *ZNW* 6 (1905) 80-101; F. C. Grant, *Ancient Judaism and the New Testament* (Edinburgh, 1960) 110, 112; McKenzie, *op. cit.*, 575.

106. S. Muñoz Iglesias, "El Género literario del Evangelio de la Infancia en San Mateo," *EstBib* 17 (1958) 243-73; M. Bourke, "The Literary Genus of Matthew 1-2," *CBQ* 22 (1960) 160-75.

of the NT—texts which are simply applied to a new situation. Moreover, these five texts are not the only citations in the narrative. There are some implicit citations from the LXX of Ex (Mt 2, 20 from Ex 4, 19 and perhaps Mt 2, 13f. from Ex 2, 15), as well as allusions to the Moses birth story as found in biblical and extra-biblical accounts. These other biblical and non-biblical texts also shaped the narrative as well as the five explicit citations, and all (explicit citations, implicit citations and allusions) seem to be used not to direct attention to OT material so that it might be explained but to explain the person of Jesus. Hence, in fact, Mt's narrative does not seem to be midrash.

In what literary genre are our narratives written? Because of the comparisons being made between old and new and the fact that the true significance of the new is an enigma to be discovered by meditation, Laurentin speaks of the Lucan narrative as a *mashal* [107] and the same category could be suggested for Mt 1-2 on the same grounds. The suggestion is no more satisfactory than the classification midrash. *Mashal* has its own range of meanings within biblical literature, none of which is this new and modern denotation. Whatever else may be said of OT *mashal*, it is certain that when it does represent a parable/allegory/extended comparison, it is regularly the anterior, lesser, prototypical term of the comparison which is described in a self-consistent manner and in detail, and it is the subsequent, primary, typified term which is left for the reader/hearer to fill out from those data. Our material does the exact opposite. Perhaps the best classification of our material is simply *infancy narrative,* for these chapters seem to have been written in

---

107. Laurentin, *op. cit.,* 117-18.

the tradition of infancy stories, biblical and extra-biblical, sharing with them many of their motifs. [108]   The Jewish stories of biblical figures were of a composite genre, midrashic infancy stories, because they were at the same time embellishments on the biblical text.   The NT stories are not midrashic.

---

108. S. Muñoz Iglesias, "Los Evangelios de la Infancia y las infancias de los héroes," *EstBib* 16 (1957) 5-36; M. S. Enslin, "The Christian Stories of the Nativity," *JBL* 59 (1940) 317-38; Vermes, *op. cit.* (see n. 37) 90-95; etc. — L. Cerfaux and J. Cambier (*VDBS* 5, 590-91) suggest that the literary genre of the infancy narratives of Mt and Lk is "l'histoire populaire."

Conclusion

The word midrash in biblical studies today has come to possess two connotations: it is used on the one hand to designate a method of exegesis (a creative and actualizing handling of the biblical text) and on the other as the name of a literary genre. Both usages are legitimate borrowings from the rabbinic vocabulary, but they must be kept distinct, else in classifying literary works into genres we will not delineate really similar groups of literature, for distinction in genre is something more basic than the methods employed within it, and the creative and actualizing handling of biblical material can produce works of various genres.

As the name of a literary genre, the word midrash designates a composition which seeks to make a text of Scripture from the past understandable, useful and relevant for the religious needs of a later generation. It is, thus, a literature about a literature. Midrashim exist in three forms, exegetical, homiletic and narrative, and they are accomplished in two ways: explicitly (the biblical text is presented and additional homiletic material and comments are assembled at the side of the biblical text) and implicitly (the interpretative material is worked into the text by means of a paraphrase).

Examples of midrash in the pre-rabbinic literature include the Midrash of the Passover Haggadah, the Qumrân *pᵉšārîm,* the Biblical Antiquities of Pseudo-Philo, the homilies in Wis 11-19 and Jn 6, and probably the Genesis Apocryphon.

In addition, isolated midrashic sections occur in the Palestinian targums and in works of other genres in connection with explicit and implicit biblical citations. However, an implicit or explicit citation from Scripture does not of itself indicate that the surrounding passage is midrashic, for the text may be merely contributing to the new composition. Only if the new composition contributes something by way of understanding to the text cited is the composition midrash. In the same connection, the mere citation of a text of Scripture in a specific sense is not a midrash. An interpretation of the original text has taken place in the mind of the author, but the composition that he writes does not interpret it and therefore the composition is not midrashic.

Just as context is a determining factor of literary form in the case of parable and allegory, so also with midrash. A midrash is always explicitly or implicitly placed in the context of the biblical text(s) upon which it comments. Works like Chr and JA which rework biblical material in what appears to be the same manner as GA are not midrash because these works are not to be read in the context of previous biblical texts. They are not a literature about a literature; they are works of history which exist for their own sake. Likewise, works of didactic fiction which are not placed by the author in the context of a biblical text are not midrash. If we are to be precise in our classification of literary genres, we should borrow from the rabbis the term haggadah as well as the term midrash and use the term haggadah to describe works of didactic fiction.

Anthological style does not necessarily make a composition midrash. It can be employed to create a composition that focuses attention on earlier texts and elucidates them (midrash); it can also be used in a non-midrashic manner to contribute vocabulary, images and the biblical atmosphere to a new work of any genre.

Redaction is not to be confused with midrash. Redaction is a process or a stage in the production of a work of any genre; midrash is a composition with specific characteristics. Frequently, redaction and the writing of a midrash are undertaken for identical motives but the work resulting from redaction is not thereby a midrash. Glosses should not be classified as midrash, for they are really successive additions which intentionally or accidentally have become part of the sacred text and are absorbed by the literary form of that text.

Apocalyptic and midrash are distinct literary forms, but an apocalyptic work or a section of it can at the same time be a midrash if it manifests the primary characteristics of that genre by interpreting a sacred text of the past and showing its relevance for a later situation and a later age.

A Select Bibliography

Alonso-Schökel, L. "Genera litteraria," *Verbum Domini* 38 (1960) 3-15.

Bacher, W. *Die Agada der babylonischen Amoräer.* Strassburg: Karl Trübner, 1878.

————. *Die Agada der palästinensischen Amoräer.* 3 vols. Strassburg: Karl Trübner, 1892-99.

————. *Die Agada der Tannaiten.* 2 vols. Strassburg: Karl Trübner, 1884-90.

————. *Die älteste Terminologie der jüdischen Schriftauslegung.* Leipzig: J. C. Hinrichs, 1899.

————. *Die Bibel - und traditionsexegetische Terminologie der Amoräer.* Leipzig: J. D. Hinrichs, 1905.

————. *Die exegetische Terminologie der jüdischen Traditionsliteratur.* 2 vols. Leipzig: J. C. Hinrichs, 1899-1905.

Bloch, R. "Écriture et tradition dans le judaïsme, aperçus sur l'origine du midrash," *Cahiers Sioniens,* 8 (1954), 9-34.

————. "Midrash," *Dictionnaire de la Bible, Supplément.* Vol. 5 Paris: Letouzey et Ané, 1957. Cols. 1263-81.

Borgen, P. *Bread From Heaven.* Leiden: Brill, 1965.

Braude, W. G. *The Midrash on Psalms.* Yale Judaica Series. Vol. XIII. New Haven: Yale University Press, 1959.

Cook, S. A. "Midrash," *Encyclopaedia Britannica,* Vol. 18. 11th ed. New York: Encyclopaedia Britannica Inc., 1911. Pp. 419-23.

Ehrenpreis, I. *The "Types Approach" to Literature.* New York: Kings Crown Press, 1945.

Fitzmyer, J. A. "The Use of Explicit Old Testament Quotations in Qumran Literature and in the New Testament," *New Testament Studies,* 7 (1960-61), 297-333.

————. *The* Genesis Apocryphon *of Qumran Cave I. A Commentary.* Rome: Pontifical Biblical Institute, 1966.

Frankel, I. *Peshat in Talmudic and Midrashic Literature.* Toronto: La Salle Press, 1956.

Freedman, H., and Simon, M. (edd.). *Midrash Rabbah.* 9 vols. London: Soncino Press, 1951.

Geiger, A. *Urschrift und Übersetzungen der Bibel in ihrer Abhängigkeit von der innern Entwicklung des Judenthums.* Breslau: Hainauer, 1857.

Gertner, M. "Terms of Scriptural Interpretation: A Study in Hebrew Semantics," *Bulletin of the School of Oriental and African Studies, University of London,* 25 (1962) 1-27.

Hammill, L. *Biblical Interpretation in the Apocrypha and Pseudepigrapha.* Unpublished dissertation, University of Chicago, 1950.

Heinemann, I. *Darkê ha-Aggadah* (The Methods of the Aggadah). 2d ed. Jerusalem: The Hebrew University Press, 1954.

Heller, B. "Agadische Literatur," *Encyclopaedia Judaica.* Vol. 1. Berlin: Verlag Eschkol A.-G., 1928. cols. 979-1036.

Horovitz, S. "Midrash," *The Jewish Encyclopedia.* Vol. 8. New York: Funk and Wagnalls, 1904. Pp. 548-50.

Kadushin, M. *Organic Thinking: A Study in Rabbinic Thought.* New York: Jewish Theological Seminary, 1938.

————. *The Rabbinic Mind.* New York: Jewish Theological Seminary, 1952.

Lauterbach, J. Z. *Mekilta de-Rabbi Ishmael.* 3 vols. Philadelphia: Jewish Publication Society of America, 1933-35.

————. "Midrash Halakah," The *Jewish Encyclopedia.* Vol 8. New York: Funk and Wagnalls, 1904. Pp. 569-72.

Seeligmann, I. L. "Voraussetzungen der Midrashchexegese," *Congress Volume, Copenhagen.* Supplements to Vetus Testamentum, vol. 1. Leiden: Brill, 1953. Pp. 150-81.

Strack, H. L. *Introduction to the Talmud and Midrash.* Reprint of English translation of 1931. New York: Meridian, 1959.

Theodor, J. "Midrash Haggadah," *The Jewish Encyclopedia.* Vol. 8. New York: Funk and Wagnalls, 1904. Pp. 550-69.

_____. "Midrashim, Smaller," *The Jewish Encyclopedia*.   Vol. 8. New York: Funk and Wagnalls, 1904.   Pp. 572-80.

Thyen, H. *Der Stil der jüdisch-hellenistischen Homilie.*   Göttingen: Vandenhoek und Ruprecht, 1955.

Vermes, G. *Scripture and Tradition in Judaism.*   Leiden: Brill, 1961.

Weingreen, J. "The Rabbinic Approach to the Study of the Old Testament," *Bulletin of the John Rylands Library*, 34 (1951-52), 166-90.

Wellek, R., and Warren, A. *Theory of Literature.* 3rd ed. New York: Harcourt, Brace and World, 1962.

Zunz, L. *Die Gottesdienstlichen Vorträge der Juden.*   2d ed. by N. Brüll. Frankfurt: J. Kauffmann, 1892.

Index

INDEX OF MODERN SCHOLARS

INDEX OF REFERENCES

a) Biblical

Citation	To be Found on Page	Citation	To be Found on Page
5, 21ff.	116	*1 Timothy*	
		1, 4	36, 40
Mark		6, 4	40
4, 1-22	114		
		2 Timothy	
Luke		2, 23	40
1-2	20, 139-142		
1, 46-55	122	*Titus*	
1, 68-79	119, 122	3, 9	40
1, 76-79	114		
		Hebrews	
John		3, 7-4, 11	111
6	58, 103-104,	7, 1-10	108, 111
	144	7, 11-28	111
Acts		*James*	
7	100		114
18, 15	40		
23, 29	40	*Apocalypse*	
25, 19	40		138
26, 3	40	1, 1	30
Romans			
4, 1-25	104	b) Qumrân Literature	
1 Corinthians		*CD*	
1, 18-2, 14	111	1, 13-14	117
9, 8-12	111	1, 18	40
10, 1-13	108, 111	2, 14-3, 19	99-100
15, 56	118, 125	4, 2-4	111
		4, 12-19	110-111
2 Corinthians		5, 15-18	116
3, 7-18	111	6, 4-11	111
		6, 7	40
Galatians		6, 11-14	117
3, 6-29	104	7, 12-8, 2	111
4, 21-31	111	7, 18	40
		8, 10-12	111
Ephesians			
4, 8-14	111		

Citation	To be Found on Page
De sacrificiis Abelis et Caini 76-87	103
De somniis II, 17-30	103
Legum allegoriae III, 65-75a. 162-168. 169-173	103

INDEX OF SUBJECTS